Sind Barth
7a

MATERIALS FOR LANGUAGE TEACHING AT RUDOLF STEINER (WALDORF) SCHOOLS

The Flying Enterprise

The Ship That Turned Over

Retold and annotated by Peter Morris
Illustrated by Christiane Lesch

edition waldorf

Herausgeber:
Pädagogische Forschungsstelle beim Bund der Freien Waldorfschulen,
Wagenburgstraße 6, 70184 Stuttgart

Sie finden uns im Internet unter
www.waldorfbuch.de

2. Auflage 2007

ISBN 978-3-927286-84-9

Gesamtherstellung:
Druck- und Medienzentrum Gerlingen GmbH,
Benzstraße 8, 70839 Gerlingen

Contents

Chapter 1
The Storm Begins

It was December 24th, 1951 – Christmas Eve. Out in the Atlantic Ocean the weather was icy-cold, and a strong wind was blowing. In this icy weather, a ship was sailing on her way from Hamburg to New York. She was carrying a lot of cargo, and a big crew of forty-three men. But there were also eleven passengers who were travelling to America. Among them were four women and two children.

It was late afternoon and the passengers were in the dining-room with the ship's officers, singing Christmas carols. The candles were burning on the Christmas tree, and they had just finished the old song, *Silent Night, Holy Night,* when one of the crew came in. He gave the captain a piece of paper.

The captain became very serious. "I'm sorry, but this is a storm warning," he told the passengers. "I must ask you to go to your cabins. The storm will be a bad one, but we'll be safe."

During the night the weather got slowly worse. The wind blew and it blew. The passengers were worried. "This isn't just a strong wind," one of them said. "It's a gale."

"Yes," said another passenger. "It's a terrible gale. And it's growing even stronger. Do you think we'll get to America safely?"

Up went the bows of the ship, down went the bows of the ship. High waves battered her sides and tossed her to and fro. Water splashed over her decks as she rolled from side to side.

All night, the wind blew harder. By the next morning, Christmas Day, 1951, it was a terrible storm. Enormous waves tossed and battered the ship without stopping, and she rolled wildly from side to side.

Suddenly, at about two o'clock in the afternoon, there was an ear-splitting noise. It was even louder than the noise of the storm.

One of the crew came running to the captain.

"Captain," he said, "the ship has cracked! She's cracked across the middle!"

Chapter 2
The Crack Gets Wider

The captain hurried down to the hold to see the crack. It went right across the deck and down the sides of the ship to sea-level. Could the sailors mend it, and could they stop the water coming in? The captain talked quietly to the first engineer.

Now the passengers were very worried. When the captain came up from the hold, some of them ran to him with questions.

"What's going to happen to us?"

"Do you think we'll get to America safely?"

"Will the storm soon be over?"

"Are we going to sink? Will we all be drowned?"

To all these questions the captain said, "Keep calm. This is a terrible storm, but we must all keep calm."

"Can you mend the crack?" asked the passengers.

"We're trying," said the captain. "The crew are doing their best."

Down in the hold, sailors were working hard to repair the crack. It was a very difficult job.

The storm went on and on. Now it was the early morning of December 27th. Many of the passengers had been in their cabins since Christmas Eve. They couldn't eat anything, because the storm had made them terribly seasick.

Now the weather grew even worse. The crack began to open wider and wider. Soon some parts of the ship were full of water. The crew couldn't stop the water coming in!

The ship was so heavy now, with all the water inside her, that the steering broke! "We can't steer the ship any more," the crew told

"Down in the hold, sailors were working hard to repair the crack."

the captain. The ship drifted helplessly in the wind and water.

The storm was now a real hurricane. In the high winds, the waves grew bigger and bigger. One enormous wave, fifteen metres high, hit the ship, and she rolled over to one side. Over, over she went. Down in the hold, part of the cargo came loose and began to roll about. It crashed against the ship's side.

Some of the passengers and crew fell over.

Another gigantic wave hit the ship.

But this time the ship didn't roll back to the other side. All the loose cargo and the water in her hold were on the same side now, so she couldn't roll back. She lay, tipped to one side, drifting in the stormy ocean.

Chapter 3

'SOS! – SOS!'

"I can't stand up," said one of the passengers.

"The deck isn't flat any more – it's as steep as the roof of a house," said another passenger. "Do you think the ship will turn right over?"

It was Friday, December 28th. The radio operator had already sent out messages to other ships nearby. Now, at half past three in the afternoon, came the most important message. "SOS! – SOS! This is the *Flying Enterprise!* We can't steer the ship. Water is coming into the hold and the ship is listing to one side. We're sinking!"

There were three other ships not too far away. When they heard the SOS message, they turned and sailed towards the *Flying Enterprise* as fast as they could. But when they reached her, they had to wait. The storm was so bad that they could do nothing.

But the next morning, the weather grew a little better. The winds were not so strong now. The other ships began to pump oil onto the water, and soon it lay all round the *Flying Enterprise* in a black pool, covering the waves and calming them down. The captain of the *Flying Enterprise* told all the people on board, "Everyone must leave the ship now. But we're listing so badly that we can't use the lifeboats. I'm afraid you'll have to jump."

So everyone put on their lifejackets and the first passengers jumped, together with the ship's cook. The water was like ice. Motorboats from the other ships were waiting, and quickly they picked up the people from the oily water.

The wind blew as the boats went back and forth through the waves. First they took the cold, wet people over to the other ships, then they came back to the *Flying Enterprise* and waited to pick up the next people to jump into the black, icy water.

It took a long time. Finally, at ten past five in the afternoon, they picked up the last of the crew.

"Where's the captain?" the sailors on the other ships asked. "He's still on the *Flying Enterprise,*" said the crew. "But she'll sink soon," the sailors said, surprised. "The captain doesn't think she'll sink," replied the crew.

They looked over the stormy sea at the *Flying Enterprise.* There they could see the captain. He was standing on the deck – alone.

"What's his name?" someone asked.

"Captain Carlsen," was the answer.

Chapter 4
Captain Carlsen Alone

Captain Carlsen was alone on the *Flying Enterprise* on the stormy waters of the Atlantic Ocean. Waves were still battering the ship and breaking over the decks.

Now another ship arrived – a destroyer of the American Navy. Her name was the *Willard Keith.*

"... and waited to pick up the next people to jump into the icy water."

The sailors on board the destroyer looked over at the *Flying Enterprise.* "She's got no chance at all in this terrible weather. She'll sink soon," said one of them.

"You're right," another sailor answered. "She's listing more and more now."

"Soon the whole side of the ship will be lying in the water, and then she'll turn right over."

The *Willard Keith's* captain took a loudhailer and called to the *Flying Enterprise.* "Hullo, Captain Carlsen!" he said. "I think it's time you left your ship."

"No, thank you," replied Captain Carlsen. "I'm going to stay on the *Flying Enterprise* until she's towed to port. Or until she sinks."

The *Flying Enterprise* drifted northwards on the stormy sea. She was listing sixty degrees to the side, her steering no longer worked and she was slowly filling with water.

Meanwhile, the New Year had come: it was now January 1st, 1952, a Tuesday. The *Willard Keith* was still sailing as near to the *Flying Enterprise* as she could. The sailors on the destroyer had just heard some surprising news.

"Captain Carlsen thinks he can get his ship back to port."

"Get his ship to port? How does he think he can do that?"

"He's ordered a tug to salvage her – the *Turmoil*!"

The *Turmoil* was the most powerful ocean-going tug in the world. But at this time, she was towing another ship across the Bay of Biscay to the port of Falmouth, on the South coast of England. The next day, Wednesday, January 2nd, the *Turmoil* arrived at Falmouth with the ship that she had salvaged. After waiting only twenty minutes to pick up fresh supplies, she turned round and set course for the *Flying Enterprise.* It was two o'clock in the afternoon when she left port, and the weather was terrible. The wind was blowing at fifty miles per hour and there were heavy showers of hail.

In the North Atlantic, Captain Carlsen had been alone on his ship for five days now – wet, sleepless and hungry.

The captain of the destroyer picked up his loudhailer again. "The *Turmoil* will be here in twenty-four hours, Captain Carlsen. Are you all right?"

Two American sailors were standing on the deck of the *Willard Keith*. They looked over at the *Flying Enterprise*, and one of them said, "Oh no! Look at those waves! They're breaking right over the ship!"

"Can you see Captain Carlsen?" the other sailor asked.

"Yes, – there he is. He's holding onto a rope and waving."

"Look at the deck – it's like the roof of a house!"

Captain Carlsen was still holding onto the rope. Without this rope, he would have rolled right off the *Flying Enterprise* and into the sea. He waved to the *Willard Keith* again and then went into one of the cabins.

"Did you see that big wave?" said the first sailor. "It broke right where he was standing. That ship's going to sink soon."

Chapter 5
Cold and Thirsty

Captain Carlsen was in his cabin, but he couldn't stand on the floor. The ship was now listing so much that he had to stand on the wall of his cabin.

For six days now, there had been no electricity on the *Flying Enterprise*. But Captain Carlsen had a hobby. He loved radios – especially short-wave radios. In his cabin he had a radio of this kind, which he had built himself. It ran on batteries, and with it he could speak to the *Willard Keith*. Mostly, the weather was too bad for this radio to reach England, so now Captain Carlsen sent a special message to the American destroyer: "Please tell my wife

"The captain of the destroyer picked up his loudhailer again."

I'm all right. Tell her not to be worried about me."

Back came the answer from the destroyer's radio room: "All right. We'll contact England and tell your wife you're all right. The *Turmoil* is on her way. She'll be here soon. Good night."

The *Flying Enterprise* was rolling to almost eighty degrees in the stormy seas, and at any moment, she might turn right over. If that happened, she would sink very quickly, and the captain would go down with his ship. There would be no time to help him. So the people on the other ships were very worried about him. But Captain Carlsen seemed to have nerves of steel.

Night fell, and the wind grew stronger. Huge waves began to batter the ship again. Half full of water, the *Flying Enterprise* drifted helplessly in the heavy seas.

None of the electric lights worked now, so the captain looked for a candle. Finally, he found one and lit it. All the time, the badly listing ship was going up and down, up and down, in the storm. The captain couldn't sleep much, because he had to watch his ship.

When will the *Turmoil* get here? he thought. How far am I from England now?

He was cold and thirsty. He couldn't make any hot tea to drink, because he couldn't boil any water. So he had to do without tea. He found some cold lemonade and drank it slowly.

Finally, morning came. The wind was still blowing hard, and huge waves were washing over the decks. The captain sent a radio message to the *Willard Keith:* "How far am I from England?"

The destroyer radioed back: "You're 350 miles from England. The tug will be here soon. Can you hold on a bit longer?"

"Yes, I can," replied Captain Carlsen. "I'm going to hold on till the *Turmoil* arrives or till the ship sinks."

"Tell my wife not to be worried about me."

Chapter 6
Warm Food and Drink

The hours went by, and still the sea was stormy. It was Thursday, January 3rd and the weather was icy. Alone on his ship, Captain Carlsen still had nothing hot to eat or drink.

"It's so cold! Let's send Captain Carlsen something hot to warm him up," said the men on the American destroyer.

But they couldn't get near the *Flying Enterprise,* so how could they send him any warm food or a hot drink?

On board the destroyer, the sailors had a special kind of gun, which could help ships in trouble. This gun could shoot a rope across the water to another ship. So the American sailors went to the gun and fired it.

The rope flew across the waves, and fell on the deck of the *Flying Enterprise.*

Captain Carlsen tried to catch it. But his ship was listing so much that the decks sloped very steeply. It was hard to scramble along them. He missed the rope, and it fell into the water.

"Let's try again," said the sailors on the *Willard Keith.* But the second rope and the third were both blown away by the strong winds, and fell into the sea.

The fourth time they fired the gun, Captain Carlsen caught the rope and tied it to a rail.

Now the American sailors tied a box to the rope. The *Flying Enterprise* drifted helplessly in the wild seas as the box hung and swung over the waves. Slowly, the captain pulled the box towards him. At last, it swung near to the place where Captain Carlsen was standing. He reached out and caught it.

"Hurray!" shouted the sailors on the *Willard Keith.* The captain waved his cap to them, full of thanks. Then, with the box, he scrambled along the deck to his cabin.

"Captain Carlsen caught the rope and tied it to a rail."

In his cabin, he stood on the wall. After opening the box, he drank some hot coffee – his first for a week! Then he ate some sand-wiches and sweets, and looked at the magazines which they had sent.

The American sailors gazed across the stormy sea at the *Flying Enterprise.* "He must be feeling very cold," said one of the sailors. "It's time the captain had a good meal."

"Look at the ship's funnel," said another sailor. "It's nearly in the water. And when the sea water runs into it, the ship will turn over."

"Let's hope the *Turmoil* arrives soon!"

Chapter 7

The *Turmoil* Starts Work

"The tug's coming! The tug's coming!" The sailors on the destroyer all cheered. It was eight o'clock on Thursday evening, and Captain Carlsen was wet and tired after six long days and nights alone on the *Flying Enterprise.* But he too was happy.

The wind had died down a little in the afternoon, but it was growing worse again now. The rain, too, was heavier. In weather like this, it was going to be difficult for the tug to get a rope to the *Flying Enterprise.* And they had to get a rope to her so that they could tow her along.

The *Turmoil* was English – the most powerful ocean-going tug in the world. She was much, much smaller than the *Flying Enterprise* or the American destroyer, but her engines were immensely strong and she had modern equipment.

Because the situation was so bad, the crew of the *Turmoil* began work immediately. It was dark, of course, but the *Turmoil* had big, strong lights. With a special rope-gun like the one that the

American sailors had used, it was easy to shoot a rope over to Captain Carlsen's ship. But this rope was much too thin and weak to tow a big ship. They would have to tie a thicker, stronger rope to the end of the first one. And to the end of this thicker rope they would have to tie a heavy steel cable. Then Captain Carlsen would have to pull this heavy steel cable across the sea and up onto his ship. But the captain had to hold onto the ship with one hand all the time, because the *Flying Enterprise* was listing so badly. So he only had one hand to pull the heavy cable with. If he tried to work with both hands, he would fall overboard. The crew of the *Turmoil* could see that the ship was very low in the water. At the back end of the big ship – the stern –, the broken rudder was above the waves.

"It's going to be very hard for Captain Carlsen, alone," said the captain of the tug to his mate. "Yes," said the mate, whose name was Mr Dancy. "He needs help."

Slowly, the tug sailed nearer to the *Flying Enterprise.* "Look, there's Captain Carlsen, holding onto the rails."

"The ship's nearly lying on her side. Do you think we can get her to England?"

"We can try. But first we've got to fix the cable between her and us. It won't be easy."

Chapter 8

A Helper for the Captain

In the night, they tried twice to get a rope to Captain Carlsen, but they couldn't. Early on Friday morning, they began again. They tried five times at the front end of the ship, but nothing worked. Then they moved round to the other end of the big ship – the stern – and began to try there.

The two ships swung up and down in the stormy sea. The *Flying Enterprise* was almost on her side, her funnel close to the water now. Next to her, the *Turmoil* looked tiny as she sailed nearer and nearer.

A man at the front of the tug aimed the rope-gun and fired. The rope flew over the *Flying Enterprise.* Captain Carlsen tried to catch it, but he had to hold onto the rail at the same time. He couldn't catch the rope with only one hand.

"He can't catch it by himself," said a sailor. "And even if he does, he can't tie it with one hand."

"He must have some help," said the captain of the tug to his mate, Mr Dancy.

"I'll help him," said Mr Dancy. "If there's a chance to get on board ..."

Now another rope flew over the ship's stern. But Captain Carlsen missed it again.

The tug was close to the *Flying Enterprise* now. Then something happened that seemed impossible.

A wave lifted the *Turmoil* up. *Bang!* She bumped against the *Flying Enterprise.* The stern rail was only two metres above the men on the tug's deck.

Mr Dancy saw his chance and jumped. With both hands, he grabbed the rail! In seconds, the seas had moved the two ships apart again. Mr Dancy hung and swung from the *Flying Enterprise's* stern, climbing up as the waves broke over him.

With a final jump, he landed on board the ship.

Holding on tight, he scrambled up the deck.

"I'm Kenneth Dancy. Pleased to meet you!" he said.

"Kurt Carlsen," said the tired captain, smiling at the man who had risked his life to help him. The two men shook hands. Captain Carlsen wasn't alone any longer.

"Mr Dancy hung and swung from the *Flying Enterprise's* stern."

Chapter 9
Working in the Storm

Now there were two men on board the *Flying Enterprise.* It was the afternoon of Friday, January 4th. The wind was blowing at forty miles per hour, and slowly, fog was beginning to close in around them.

Again and again, the tug fired a rope over to the listing ship; again and again, the rope slipped off in the heavy seas before the two men could reach it. Once, the rope fell right next to them, and they managed to catch it. They tried to tie it to the stern. But the ship was moving and shaking so much in the storm that the rope soon slipped off. All the time, enormous waves came crashing onto the ship, and water washed around them. Finally, it grew dark.

"Come on," said Captain Carlsen.

The two men scrambled along the steeply sloping deck and climbed through the door of the captain's cabin. Mr Dancy saw the hammock where the captain had tried to get a little sleep. In it there was some cake. Mr Dancy's eyes lit up.

"I'm sorry, but there's nothing to eat now except this. Do you like cake?" asked Captain Carlsen.

"Oh yes, I love cake," said Mr Dancy.

"We can hang up a hammock for you here," said the captain. "And here's a lifejacket for you."

Kenneth Dancy put on the lifejacket.

The two men sat and talked as the evening went on, and they both ate some cake by the light of a candle. All the time, the ship listed a little more and her funnel moved a little nearer to the water as she drifted in the heavy seas.

In the morning, the fog had cleared. As soon as it was light, the tug tried again to shoot a rope to the men on the *Flying Enterprise.*

Sometimes the rope slipped off into the water, as on the day before. Once, the weight of the steel cable was too heavy for the two men and they had to let it go. Finally, at twenty to ten that Saturday morning, Captain Carlsen and Mr Dancy managed to pull the heavy steel towing-cable across to their ship and fasten it to the stern.

"Hurray!" cheered the sailors on the tug. The two men's hands were bleeding, but they waved back.

The *Turmoil* began to sail away. Slowly, the long steel towing-cable grew tight, pulling the *Flying Enterprise* along behind it.

"Well – we're on our way to England," said one of the crew on board the tug. "But will we get there with the *Flying Enterprise*?"

Chapter 10
The Cable Breaks

The two ships sailed eastwards at a speed of three knots – about as fast as you would normally walk. In these stormy seas, the *Flying Enterprise* might sink more quickly if they tried to move faster. But if they travelled too slowly, she would sink anyway, before they could reach port in England.

The *Turmoil* sailed along in front; behind her, at the end of almost 700 metres of steel cable, the *Flying Enterprise* moved slowly along on her side, stern-first.

Several days passed while the ships continued slowly. The weather grew a little better, but it was still bad. In the North Atlantic in winter, the weather is never good. But now, at least, the wind was not so strong, and the waves were not as high as before.

The *Willard Keith* sailed along beside them. Sometimes it shot a rope over to the *Flying Enterprise*. This was easier now that the weather wasn't so stormy. With this rope, the sailors could send a box of food and hot drinks to the two men on the other ship.

A helicopter flew out from England, carrying newspaper reporters from England and from Denmark. Captain Carlsen lived in America now, but he came from Copenhagen, and all the Danes were very proud of him. The helicopter circled over the ships while the reporters took photographs; then it flew away again. Later, a plane came over, took photographs and flew away.

And all the time, water was slowly filling the *Flying Enterprise* through the crack in her sides.

Newspapers were full of stories about the 'DRAMA ON THE HIGH SEAS'. In those days, not many people had television, but millions listened to the radio. And on the radio, too, there was a lot of talk about the *Flying Enterprise.*

"Will the *Flying Enterprise* get to England? We have two experts here in the studio who are going to discuss the question. The first thinks she'll manage it; but the second says she has no chance."

Everyone agreed that Captain Carlsen was really one of the bravest men they had ever heard of. And so was Mr Dancy.

But out in the Atlantic, the weather was getting worse again. Hour by hour, the wind grew stronger and the waves rose higher, crashing against the ship. On Tuesday, January 8th, the *Flying Enterprise* was listing eighty degrees to the side. It was now two weeks since the accident and the funnel was only a few metres from the water.

And there was another problem. Because the ship was now listing so badly, the steel towing-cable at the stern was rubbing over sharp metal. Would the cable hold?

Every two hours, Captain Carlsen or Mr Dancy scrambled along the steeply sloping deck to look at it. Once, Captain Carlsen took a pound of butter with him and smeared it on the cable. He felt a bit silly as he did so, but he thought it might help. He didn't want the cable to break.

"Suddenly – *snap!* – the cable broke."

Every time they scrambled along the deck, the men got wet through. Back in the cabin, they tried to dry their clothes. But they only had candles to help them, so their clothes stayed wet.

"We're making good progress," the crew of the *Turmoil* reported to England.

"Making good progress," reported the American destroyer. "Good old Captain Carlsen!" said everyone in England and America and Denmark.

The King of Denmark said, "We must give Captain Carlsen a medal for his bravery." The Danish government ordered a special plane to fly the medal to England. There it was taken to Falmouth, on the South coast. That was the port the ships were heading for.

Slowly, very slowly, the tug came on, towing the *Flying Enterprise* behind her. They were now a hundred miles away from England. After another while, they were just eighty miles from England. Then they had only sixty miles to go.

Over the radio came a weather report: "The weather will soon get much worse, with more gales and heavy rain."

Night came on. The wind blew harder and harder. But Captain Carlsen and Mr Dancy couldn't sleep – they kept going outside to look at the cable. Huge waves washed round them and they had to hold on tight as they moved along the decks. Suddenly – *snap!* – the cable broke.

Chapter 11

The Storm Gets Worse

It was half past one in the morning of Wednesday, January 9th. The *Flying Enterprise* was only fifty-three miles from Falmouth. Everything was dark, and the waves were big and black. The tug sent a radio message: "We'll have to wait for daylight."

The *Flying Enterprise* was helpless, and she was drifting away from England. The *Turmoil* couldn't stop her.

When morning came, Mr Dancy looked at the funnel. Yes, it was now only just above the waves. The ship was taking on more and more water. The tug came nearer and shot a rope across to the *Flying Enterprise.* But waves were breaking all across the ship's decks, and the two men couldn't reach the rope. It seemed impossible.

The captain and crew of the *Turmoil* tried again and again, but the weather was now too bad. In the heavy seas, the *Flying Enterprise* drifted to the west – away from Falmouth.

Night came on again, and the gale grew even worse. Captain Carlsen and Mr Dancy couldn't stay in their cabin because now the water was washing in. They moved to another cabin, higher up the deck.

The door of this cabin was above their heads. It was like having a door in the ceiling. The wind went on blowing, and all the time, more water was washing into the *Flying Enterprise,* and she was sinking lower and lower in the sea.

The next morning, January 10th, Mr Dancy climbed up a rope to get out of the cabin. He saw that the first waves were breaking into the funnel. He went back down the rope and told Captain Carlsen.

"It's almost time for us to go," said the captain.

Chapter 12
The Ship Sinks

They sent a message to both the *Turmoil* and the American destroyer, the *Willard Keith:* "We're abandoning ship."

The rain beat down and the ship sank lower. The funnel was dipping in the water now. The gale was terribly strong. The two

"Quickly, helping hands pulled them from the ice-cold waters."

men had to climb up higher and higher on the ship. They had to get away from the waves as fast as they could. "Come on," said Captain Carlsen to Mr Dancy. They climbed along the funnel. At the end of the funnel, the water was now rushing in fast. The ship had turned right over onto her side.

Captain Carlsen and Mr Dancy stood on the funnel. The captain wanted to be the last to leave the ship. So, at twenty-four minutes past three, Mr Dancy jumped into the icy sea. One minute later, Captain Carlsen followed him into the water.

"Bad luck, Captain!" called Mr Dancy. "We did everything we could!" Captain Carlsen shouted back. Quickly, helping hands pulled them from the ice-cold waters, and only five minutes later, they were on board the *Turmoil.*

"The *Flying Enterprise* is right on her side now. She's going down ... She's going down. The waves are breaking over her. She's tipping up her bows ... She's going ... going ... She's gone!"

It was ten past four on the afternoon of Thursday, January 10th, 1952. Captain Carlsen had fought for his ship for fourteen days, but she had died at last.

When the *Turmoil* sailed into the port of Falmouth that evening, crowds of people shouted, while horns and sirens sounded from all the boats round them. But Kurt Carlsen and Ken Dancy didn't hear a thing. They were down in the *Turmoil's* cabins, fast asleep!

Songs

Blow, Boys, Blow

2. And how do you know she's a Yankee clipper?
Blow, boys, blow.
Her masts and sails shine out like silver,
Blow, my bully boys, blow.

3. This Yankee ship is bound for China,
Blow, boys, blow.
The Stars and Stripes stream out behind her,
Blow, my bully boys, blow.

4. And what do you think they had for dinner?
Blow, boys, blow.
'Twas water soup, but slightly thinner,
Blow, my bully boys, blow.

5. Oh, blow, my boys, and blow together,
Blow, boys, blow.
Oh, blow, my boys, for better weather,
Blow, my bully boys, blow.

6. Oh, blow today and blow tomorrow,
Blow, boys, blow.
We'll blow away all care and sorrow,
Blow, my bully boys, blow.

Blow, You Winds in the Morning

2. They send you to New Bedford town, that famous whaling port,
   And hand you to some landsharks there to board and fit you out,
   singing
   Blow, you winds ...

3. And now we're out to sea, my boys, the wind comes on to blow;
   And half the crew is sick on deck, the other below,
   singing
   Blow, you winds ...

4. When we get home, our ship made fast, and we are through with sailing,
   A brimming glass around we'll pass and never more go whaling,
   singing
   Blow, you winds ...

The Leaving of Liverpool

2. I'm off to California,
By the way of the stormy Cape Horn,
And I will send to you a letter, love,
When I am homeward bound.
So fare you well ...

3. Farewell to Lower Frederick Street,
Anson Terrace and Park Lane,
Farewell, it will be some long time
Before I see you again.
So fare you well ...

4. I've joined a British clipper ship,
From the town I know so well,
And Burgess is her captain's name,
But they say she's a floating hell.
So fare you well ...

5. The tug is waiting at the pierhead
To take us down the stream,
Our sails are loose and our anchor's secure,
So I'll bid you goodbye, my dear.
So fare you well ...

6. I'm bound away to leave you,
With just one thing on my mind:
The only thing that grieves me,
Is leaving you behind.
So fare you well ...

The Beaufort Scale of Wind

Beaufort number	*Description of wind*	*Effects of wind / Description of sea surface*	*Wind speed (kph)*	*Wave height (metres)*
0	Calm	Smoke rises vertically; sea like a mirror; unruffled	< 1	0
1	Light air	Direction shown by smoke drift, but not by weather-vanes. Ripples with appearance of scales are formed, without foam crests	1–5	0
2	Light breeze	Wind felt on face; leaves rustle; weather-vanes move. Small wavelets; still short,but more pronounced; crests have a glassy appearance but do not break	6–11	0–0.3
3	Gentle breeze	Leaves and twigs in motion; light flag extended. Large wavelets; crests begin to break; foam of glassy appearance; perhaps scattered white horses	12–19	0.3–0.6
4	Moderate breeze	Dust and small paper raised; small branches moved. Small waves becoming longer; fairly frequent white horses	20–28	0.6–1.2
5	Fresh breeze	Small trees in leaf begin to sway. Crests form on waves; many white horses; chance of some spray	29–38	1.2–2.4
6	Strong breeze	Large branches in motion; telegraph wires hum. Large waves begin to form; white foam crests more extensive everywhere; probably some spray	39–49	2.4–4
7	Moderate gale	Whole trees in motion; walking against wind difficult. Sea heaps up, and white foam from breaking waves begins to be blown in streaks along the direction of the wind; spindrifts begin to be seen	50–61	4–6
8	Fresh gale	Twigs break off trees. Foam blown off in dense streaks; edges of crests break into spindrift	62–74	4–6

Beaufort number	*Description of wind*	*Effects of wind / Description of sea surface*	*Wind speed (kph)*	*Wave height (metres)*
9	Strong gale	Slight structural damage, chimney pots and slates fall. High waves, sea begins to roll, spray affects visibility	75–88	4–6
10	Whole gale	Trees uprooted, considerable structural damage. Very high waves with long overhanging crests, resulting foam in great patches is blown in dense white streaks; on the whole the surface of the sea takes on a white appearance; rolling of the sea becomes heavy; visibility affected	89–102	6–9
11	Storm	Widespread damage; rare inland. Sea is covered with long white patches of foam; everywhere, the edges of the wave crests are blown into foam; visibility affected	103–117	9–14
12	Hurricane	Countryside devastated; experienced only in tropical cyclones. Air is filled with foam and spray; visibility very seriously affected	> 117	> 14

The *Beaufort Wind-Force Scale* was first devised in 1805 by Admiral Sir Francis Beaufort for describing winds at sea. It was based on a scale of 13 wind strengths, as thirteen was the number of sails that a fully-rigged ship carried.

Originally, the scale had no wind speeds. Beaufort used his scale to give more exact meanings to words like *breeze*, *gale*, etc, which, until then, people had understood in different ways. This first Beaufort Scale was in use for about a hundred years.

In 1905, Sir George Simpson made some changes to the Beaufort Scale, so that seamen in steamships could use it better. He revised the definitions, giving a description of how each wind speed would affect things like smoke, leaves, and trees. He also reduced the thirteen categories to twelve.

In 1939, some small changes were made to help landsmen, and wind speeds were added, which could be measured in weather stations.

This revised version has been adopted by the International Meteorological Committee, and is now the standard to which all nations conform.

The Last Hour of the *Flying Enterprise*

The day after the *Flying Enterprise* sank, a newspaper gave this dramatic report of the ship's last hour. It came from Mr S. E. Watson, a lifeboat man who had been listening to the radio messages between all the ships (*The Daily Telegraph*, 11.1.1952).

Mr Watson told the newspaper reporter: "Shortly after 3 o'clock, I heard the captain of the *Willard Keith* telling Captain Carlsen to come off the ship. I kept hearing him say 'No.' " Then followed these messages:

3.15 pm: *Turmoil* and *Willard Keith* edging in skilfully to get close to wallowing, sinking ship.
3.16 pm: *Flying Enterprise* at 80 degrees. Carlsen and Dancy seen on starboard side of deckhouse. Warned to be ready to jump.
3.20 pm: Water now pouring down funnel of *Flying Enterprise*. Carlsen and Dancy preparing to jump from funnel.
3.25 pm: Carlsen and Dancy seen swimming in boiling seas.
3.30 pm: *Turmoil* signals: "We have rescued Carlsen and Dancy. They are OK. Now in captain's cabin getting into dry clothing."
3.31 pm: *Willard Keith* signals to *Turmoil:* "Well done."
3.32 pm: Mast of *Flying Enterprise* slapping water. Ship now beginning to break up.
3.33 pm: Ship sinking by stern. Wooden objects from decks floating around.
3.40 pm: Last moments seem to have arrived. Bows well under water. Cargo everywhere. *Flying Enterprise* still struggling up.
3.44 pm: Bows completely under the water.
3.50 pm: Going down fast by the stern.
3.53 pm: One third of the vessel still visible, but the stern cannot be seen.
4.00 pm: Last lifeboat washed off the ship.
4.01 pm: Starboard bow is just showing. The *Turmoil* has closed in a bit.
4.05 pm: The *Flying Enterprise's* funnel can still be seen. She seems to be putting up a brave show for the last minutes. Captain Carlsen now standing by rail of tug for last farewell look. Looking towards her. Now he has turned his head away. The *Turmoil* has also turned away.
4.07 pm: Flares on the *Flying Enterprise* are suddenly ignited by water, lighting the sea in the growing darkness.
4.08 pm: Bows of the *Flying Enterprise* shoot up in the air and remain aloft for some seconds.
4.09 pm: Sirens sound in farewell from the escort vessels.
4.10 pm: *Flying Enterprise* finally sinks beneath the water.

Basic Vocabulary (248 words in 17 groups)

Short forms used in the list:

opp.	–	opposite	–	*Gegensatz*
n.	–	noun	–	*Hauptwort*
pl.	–	plural	–	*Mehrzahl*
h.	–	here	–	*hier*
s.o.	–	someone	–	*jemand*
s.th.	–	something	–	*etwas*
s.	–		–	*sich*
jmd.	–		–	*jemand*
etw.	–		–	*etwas*

The following list mostly excludes the irregular verbs from the text. These are listed separately at the back of the book.

QUESTION WORDS

who	*Who* is that boy sitting next to you?	wer
what	*What* would you like: tea or coffee?	was
which	*Which* pullover should I wear: the blue one or the red one?	welche(r, s)
where	*Where* is your brother? – I don't know.	wo
where ... from	*Where* do you come *from*? – Germany.	wo ... her
where ... to	*Where* was the ship sailing *to*? – New York.	wo ... hin
when	*When* will the storm end?	wann
how	*How* far are we from England?	wie
why	*Why* haven't you done your homework?	warum

THE SHIP AND THE SEA

ship	big boat that sails on the sea	Schiff
cargo	the things that a ship carries	Ladung, Fracht(gut)
hold	A ship carries her cargo in the *hold*.	Lade-, Frachtraum
to sail	to travel on the water	segeln, fahren
bows	the front end of a ship	Bug
stern	the back end of a ship	Heck
steering	This helps you to turn left or right.	Steuer-, Ruderanlage
rudder	thing at the back of a ship to make her turn	Steuerruder
funnel	the chimney of a ship	Schornstein *(vom Schiff)*
deck	floor of a ship	Deck
rail	Round the deck there is a *rail*.	Geländer, Reling
cabin	room on a ship	Kabine
floor	part of a room where you stand and walk	Fußboden

wall	the side of a room	Wand
ceiling	part of a room over our heads	(Zimmer-)Decke
captain	the chief person on a ship	Kapitän
crew	people who work on a ship	Besatzung
sailor	one of the crew on a ship	Matrose
passenger	person who travels on a ship, a train	Fahrgast, Passagier
port	town with a place where ships can land	Hafen(stadt)
water	The sea is full of *water*.	Wasser
wave	rolling water on the sea	Welle
to splash	to make s.th. wet	*h:* spritzen
to batter	to hit hard	gegen etw. schlagen
to toss	to throw about	werfen, schleudern
to roll	The ball *rolled* under the table.	rollen
on board	on the ship	an Bord
overboard	over the side of the boat and into the water	über Bord
to be drowned	to die under water	ertrinken
lifeboat	small boat on a ship to save people if the ship sinks (to save = retten)	Rettungsboot
lifejacket	This stops you from sinking in the water.	Schwimmweste
tug	a small ship that tows other ships	Schlepper
to tow	to pull a ship, a car	(ab)schleppen
rope	a strong, thick line	Seil
to tie	to make a knot	binden, festmachen
steel	strong hard metal for knives, machines (to st*ea*l = stehlen!)	Stahl
cable	a strong, thick rope	Kabel
gun	You can shoot with this.	Gewehr
to shoot, shot, shot	to fire a gun	schießen
to fire	to shoot a gun	feuern, schießen
to aim	to point a gun at s.th.	zielen

THE WEATHER

storm	bad weather, with rain and strong winds	Sturm
weather	sunshine, wind, rain and snow	Wetter
cold	not warm; like ice or snow	kalt
hot	*opp.* cold	heiß
wet	covered with water; *opp.* dry	nass
dry	The wood will burn if it is *dry*.	trocken

to blow, blew, blown	The wind *blew* his hat off.	blasen, wehen
gale	very strong wind	Sturm(wind)
rain	water from the sky	Regen
ice	water that has become hard because it's cold	Eis
cloud	Those dark *clouds* will bring rain.	Wolke
fog	thick cloud on the ground that stops you seeing clearly	Nebel
to die down	to become weaker	nachlassen
dark	At night it is *dark*. *opp.* light	dunkel
light	It is *light* in the daytime, and dark at night.	hell

'WHEN' WORDS

when	1. *When* he went home, it was raining.	als, wenn
	2. *When* did she come? – At three o'clock.	wann
now	Come here *now*!	jetzt, nun
immediately	at once; I can't wait – we must go *immediately*.	sofort
as soon as	He went home *as soon as* school was over.	sobald
early	*opp.* late	früh
late	You mustn't be *late* for school!; *opp.* early	spät
soon	in a short time; I'll come home *soon*.	bald
since	*Since* last Monday, it has rained every day.	seit
already	before now; I've *already* told you that!	schon
first ... then	*First* think what to say, *then* say it.	als erstes ... dann
meanwhile	Jim ate supper. *Meanwhile* I did my homework.	inzwischen
until	till; Wait here *until* I come back.	bis
till	until	bis
during	*During* the night, we sleep.	während *(mit Hauptwort)*
while	The mothers talked *while* the children played.	während *(es folgt ein Verb!)*
finally	at last; After a long time, they *finally* found the lost child.	schließlich
at last	in the end, finally	schließlich; endlich
first	The *first* month is January.	erste(r, s)
last	December is the *last* month in the year.	letzte(r, s)
still	I can't go – I'm *still* doing my homework.	(immer) noch
just	at the moment: We are *just* going out.	gerade, soeben
no longer	It *no longer* works = It doesn't work any more.	nicht mehr
time	You're lazy – it's *time* you began working hard.	Zeit
It took a long time.	He walked to school, and *it took* two hours.	Es dauerte lang.

all the time	I don't like him: he talks *all the time.*	die ganze Zeit
to go by	to pass; (to go = gehen)	vorübergehen
day	The sun shines during the *day*.	Tag
night	*opp.* day	Nacht
all night	from evening till morning	die ganze Nacht hindurch
morning	the first part of the day	Morgen, Vormittag
afternoon	morning – *afternoon* – evening	Nachmittag
evening	morning – afternoon – *evening*	Abend
Christmas Eve	December 24th; the day before Christmas (Christmas = Weihnachten)	Heiliger Abend
second	There are 60 *seconds* in a minute.	Sekunde
hour	60 minutes	Stunde
week	seven days (weak = schwach!)	Woche
month	four weeks	Monat
year	There are 365 days in a *year*.	Jahr
life (pl. lives)	The old man lost his *life* in the fire.	Leben

'WHERE' WORDS

world	The Queen is one of the richest people in the *world*.	Welt
to move	This is my chair – would you *move*, please?	s. bewegen
to travel	They *travelled* from England to America.	reisen
to head for	to go towards	Kurs halten auf
to arrive	to come to a place	ankommen
to wait (for)	We *waited* at the bus-stop till the bus came.	warten (auf)
to stay	not to go away; On Sundays we *stay* at home.	bleiben
to hurry	to go (*or* to do s.th.) quickly	eilen; s. beeilen
to miss	*h:* not to catch	*h:* nicht fangen
to fall over	to fall to the ground; (to fall = fallen)	umfallen
to carry	1. Mother *carried* the baby into the garden. 2. Buses *carry* people to work.	tragen befördern, bringen
close to	(very) near to	nahe, dicht
far	*opp.* near	weit
up	Stand *up*!; *opp.* down	(hin)auf
down	The ball rolled *down* the hill; *opp:* up	(hin)unter
across	from one side to the other	(quer) über
along	from one end towards the other	entlang
between	Sit here in the middle, *between* us!	zwischen
back	Put the book *back* when you have read it.	zurück

back and forth	backwards and forwards	hin und her
to and fro	backwards and forwards	hin und her
away	from there	entfernt; weg
through	Go *through* that door and turn right!	durch
on the way to	going to (a place)	unterwegs nach
against	He fell and hit his head *against* the wall.	gegen

FEELING

serious	Stop laughing – be *serious*!; *opp.* funny	ernst
terrible	No summer holidays – that's *terrible*!	schrecklich
happy	*opp.* sad	glücklich
surprised	I'm *surprised* to see you here – I thought you were on holiday.	überrascht
surprising	S.th. not expected (= unerwartet) is *surprising*.	überraschend
brave	She was not afraid; it was *brave* of her to go into the burning house.	mutig
proud of	pleased about s.th. that s.o. has done	stolz auf
to be worried	to be afraid	beunruhigt sein, s. Sorgen machen
to keep calm	to stay quiet, not get excited (to keep = behalten)	ruhig bleiben
to smile	to have a happy look on your face	lächeln

TALKING AND LISTENING

question	what you ask	Frage
answer	I'll ask a question, and you give the answer.	Antwort
to reply	to answer; "Yes, sir," he *replied*.	antworten; erwidern
to listen to	to hear carefully; to try to hear	zuhören; horchen
to discuss	to talk about s.th.	besprechen; diskutieren
to agree	to think the same; to have the same ideas	übereinstimmen
to shout	*opp.* to speak quietly	schreien
to call	to speak loudly and clearly; to shout	rufen
to cheer	to shout "hurray!"	"hurra!" rufen

EATING AND DRINKING

food	things you can eat	Speise(n); Essen
drink	Water, milk and coffee are all *drinks*.	Getränk
to drink, drank, drunk	Babies *drink* milk.	trinken
to eat, ate eaten	He is fat because he *eats* a lot.	essen

meal	Breakfast, lunch and dinner are *meals*.	Mahlzeit
meat	beef, lamb, pork, chicken (to *meet* = treffen, begegnen!)	Fleisch
vegetable	Peas, carrots and potatoes are *vegetables*.	Gemüse(sorte)
fruit	apples, oranges, bananas	Obst; Früchte
cake	We had tea and *cakes* at five o'clock.	Kuchen
coffee	Two cups of tea and a black *coffee*, please!	Kaffee
sweets	Chocolates and toffees are *sweets*.	Bonbons, Süßigkeiten

DIFFICULTIES

in trouble	having problems	*h:* in Not
tired	The *tired* boy fell asleep quickly.	müde, ermüdet
sleepless	If you are *sleepless*, then you can't sleep.	schlaflos
to be hungry	When we *are hungry,* we want to eat s.th.	Hunger haben
to be thirsty	I'*m thirsty* – I must drink something.	Durst haben
to do without	There's no sugar, so we'll have to *do without*. (to do = tun, machen)	ohne (etw.) auskommen

BEING POLITE

Pleased to meet you!	You say this when you first meet someone. (me*a*t = Fleisch!)	Sehr erfreut, Sie kennen zu lernen!
to shake hands (with)	to give your hand to s.o. when you meet him (to shake = schütteln)	(jmd.) die Hand geben
please	Will you give me an apple, *please*?	bitte
thank you	These flowers are for you. – Oh, *thank you!*	danke
I'm sorry.	1. *I'm sorry* that your father has died. 2. *I'm sorry* – I've forgotten my homework.	Es tut mir leid ...; leider
Are you all right?	I broke my leg last year, but I'*m all right* now. (all right = in Ordnung)	Geht's Ihnen gut?
bad luck	I've lost my watch. – Oh, *bad luck*!	Pech

USEFUL WORDS

people	men, women and children	Leute, Menschen
together	Paul and I always walk to school *together*.	zusammen
quickly	I finished before you because I write *quickly*.	schnell
accident	Two people were killed in a car *accident*.	Unfall
to happen	The accident *happened* at ten past four.	geschehen, passieren
to hope	to wish that s.th. will happen	hoffen
to manage to	to be able to (do s.th. difficult)	es schaffen, etw. zu tun
to use	We *use* a pen to write with.	benutzen
to look	to seem to be: You *look* very happy today.	aussehen

to look at	Just *look at* that new car!	anschauen
to look for	to try to find; John is *looking for* a job.	suchen
to seem	That apple is bad, but this one *seems* all right.	scheinen
the same	*opp.* different	der/die/dasselbe; der/die/das gleiche
easy	I did the homework quickly because it was *easy.* (= simple); *opp.* difficult, hard	leicht
hard	difficult; *opp.* easy	schwierig
impossible	It is *impossible* for elephants to fly!	unmöglich
to be right	*opp.* to be wrong	recht haben
of course	naturally	natürlich

SMALL WORDS

a bit	a little; Let's stop – I'm *a bit* tired.	ein bisschen; ein wenig
almost	nearly; Don't go – dinner is *almost* ready.	fast, beinahe
nearly	almost; Let's go home – it's *nearly* lunchtime.	fast, beinahe
really	I had no breakfast this morning – now I'm *really* hungry!	wirklich
at least	If you forget your homework, *at least* you should say 'sorry'!	wenigstens
only	just; no more than	nur
normally	mostly; usually	normalerweise
mostly	Cows *mostly* eat grass.	meistens; hauptsächlich
too	1. That question is *too* hard – I can't answer it.	zu (sehr)
	2. Can I come *too*?	auch
except	but not: He works every day *except* Sunday.	außer
let's ...	I think that we should ... (*let's* not .../don't *let's* ... = wollen wir nicht ...)	wollen wir ...
someone	a person; *Someone* knocked at the door.	jemand
something	There's *something* on the floor – what is it?	etwas
everyone	all the people	jeder(mann)
none	not one	keine(r, s)
whose	of whom; of which; (who's = who is!)	dessen, deren; wessen
to need	We *need* water to live.	brauchen, benötigen
both	two together	beide
so that	Speak louder *so that* I can hear you!	damit

COUNTING IN ORDER

first	January is the *first* month of the year.	erste(r, s)
second	The *second* month is February.	zweite(r, s)
third	Then comes March, the *third* month.	dritte(r, s)
fourth	April is the *fourth* month.	vierte(r, s)
fifth	The *fifth* month is May.	fünfte(r, s)

COUNTING HOW OFTEN

once	one time	einmal
twice	two times	zweimal
three times	3x	dreimal
this time	I walked yesterday; *this time* I'll go by bus.	diesmal
again	once more; Never do that *again*!	wieder, nochmals
always	There is *always* a doctor in a hospital.	immer
sometimes	from time to time	manchmal
often	many times	oft
never	Children in Nigeria *never* see snow.	nie

'TO GET'

to get, got, got	1. I *got* a lot of presents for my birthday.	bekommen
	2. It *gets* dark in the evening.	werden
	3. What time will you *get* home?	(an)kommen
to get in	She *got into* her car and drove away. *opp.* to get out (of)	einsteigen
to get on	When you *get on* a bus, you need a ticket. *opp.* to get off	einsteigen

'TO BE'

(Present)		*(Past)*	
I am	ich bin	I was	ich war
you are	du bist	you were	du warst
he/she/it is	er/sie/es ist	he/she/it was	er/sie/es war
we are	wir sind	we were	wir waren
you are	ihr seid/Sie sind	you were	ihr wart/Sie waren
they are	sie sind	they were	sie waren

'TO HAVE'

(Present)		*(Past)*	
I have	ich habe	I had	ich hatte
you have	du hast	you had	du hattest
he/she/it has	er/sie/es hat	he/she/it had	er/sie/es hatte
we have	wir haben	we had	wir hatten
you have	ihr habt/Sie haben	you had	ihr hattet/Sie hatten
they have	sie haben	they had	sie hatten

Opposites and Word-Pairs

The following pairs are given whenever one of the words occurs in the text. They appear in text sequence. Some of the words are also included in the Basic Vocabulary.
In contrast to normal opposites, word pairs are not opposites in the true sense, but words often found together, such as eat *and* drink, see *and* hear, hungry *and* thirsty. *A few pairs of this kind are also included.*

Chapter 1: The Storm Begins

PAGE 3

cold	⇔	hot	kalt	⇔	heiß
strong	⇔	weak	stark	⇔	schwach
her	⇔	his	ihr	⇔	sein
from	⇔	to	von	⇔	nach, zu
a lot (of)	⇔	a little; a few	viel	⇔	ein wenig; ein paar
big	⇔	small, little	groß	⇔	klein
man (*pl.* men)	⇔	woman (*pl.* women)	Mann	⇔	Frau
late	⇔	early	spät	⇔	früh
to finish	⇔	to start, to begin	beenden	⇔	beginnen
old	⇔	new; young	alt	⇔	neu; jung
to go	⇔	to come	gehen	⇔	kommen
good	⇔	bad	gut	⇔	schlecht, schlimm
safe	⇔	in danger; dangerous	sicher	⇔	in Gefahr; gefährlich
day	⇔	night	Tag	⇔	Nacht
slow(ly)	⇔	quick(ly), fast	langsam	⇔	schnell
worse	⇔	better	schlimmer	⇔	besser
worried	⇔	calm	besorgt	⇔	gelassen
terrible	⇔	wonderful	schrecklich	⇔	wunderbar
up	⇔	down	(hin)auf	⇔	(hin)ab
bows	⇔	stern	Bug	⇔	Heck, Achterschiff
high	⇔	low	hoch	⇔	niedrig
hard	⇔	soft	hart	⇔	weich
next	⇔	last	nächste(r, s)	⇔	letzte(r, s)
enormous	⇔	tiny	riesig	⇔	winzig
suddenly	⇔	gradually	plötzlich	⇔	allmählich
about	⇔	exactly	etwa, circa	⇔	genau
loud	⇔	quiet	laut	⇔	leise

PAGE 4

to run	⇔	to walk	rennen, laufen	⇔	gehen *(im Schritt-tempo)*

Chapter 2: The Crack Gets Wider

to see	⇔	to hear	sehen	⇔	hören
to talk	⇔	to listen	reden	⇔	zuhören
quiet	⇔	noisy	leise	⇔	laut, lärmend
first	⇔	last	erste(r, s)	⇔	letzte(r, s)
now	⇔	then	jetzt, nun	⇔	dann
to sink	⇔	to swim; to float	sinken	⇔	schwimmen
this	⇔	that	diese(r, s)	⇔	jene(r, s)
these	⇔	those	diese	⇔	jene
question	⇔	answer	Frage	⇔	Antwort
calm	⇔	nervous; worried	gelassen	⇔	aufgeregt; besorgt
best	⇔	worst	beste(r, s)	⇔	schlimmste(r, s)
difficult	⇔	easy	schwierig	⇔	leicht
to go on	⇔	to stop	weitermachen	⇔	aufhören
to eat	⇔	to drink	essen	⇔	trinken
sick	⇔	well; healthy	krank	⇔	gesund
to open	⇔	to close, to shut	öffnen	⇔	schließen
wide	⇔	narrow	breit	⇔	eng
full	⇔	empty	voll	⇔	leer
in	⇔	out	ein	⇔	aus
into	⇔	out of	in ... hinein	⇔	aus ... heraus
heavy	⇔	light	schwer *(von Gewicht)*	⇔	leicht *(von Gewicht)*
inside	⇔	outside	(dr)innen	⇔	(dr)außen

PAGE 6

to fall over	⇔	to get up	umfallen	⇔	aufstehen

Chapter 3: 'SOS! – SOS!'

to stand up	⇔	to sit down	aufstehen	⇔	s. hinsetzen
roof	⇔	cellar	Dach	⇔	Keller
to send	⇔	to receive	senden	⇔	empfangen
nearby	⇔	far away	nahe	⇔	weit entfernt
most	⇔	least	meist	⇔	wenigst
towards	⇔	away from	auf ... zu	⇔	von ... weg
nothing	⇔	everything	nichts	⇔	alles

PAGE 7

black	⇔	white	schwarz	⇔	weiß

Captain Kurt Carlsen with his wife Agnes on their wedding day.

Captain Carlsen loved radios, and built one for himself. His private callsign was 'W2ZXM'. This was the radio which helped him to keep in contact with the other ships, when the *Flying Enterprise's* radio wasn't working.

The *Flying Enterprise* lists heavily to the side. This was the first photo taken from the *Turmoil*. Here the sea is still quite calm.

The first photo of the ship taken from a plane. The passengers had left the ship, but the two lifeboats are still in their places.

January 9th. Ken Dancy (*left*) and Captain Carlsen (*right*) wave from the deck of the *Flying Enterprise*.

January 9th. The cargo is slipping more and more. Water has reached the higher parts of the ship.

January 10th. At ten past four in the afternoon, the ship finally sinks.
In this photo, the stern is already under the water.

Captain Carlsen arrives in New York and is welcomed by his wife Agnes.

all	⇔	none (of)	alle	⇔	keine
everyone	⇔	no one, nobody	jedermann	⇔	niemand
to put on	⇔	to take off	anziehen	⇔	ausziehen
wet	⇔	dry	nass	⇔	trocken
long	⇔	short	lang	⇔	kurz
to ask	⇔	to answer	fragen	⇔	antworten
alone	⇔	together (with)	allein	⇔	zusammen

Chapter 4: Captain Carlsen Alone

over	⇔	under	über	⇔	unter
to arrive	⇔	to leave	ankommen	⇔	weggehen, -fahren

PAGE 9

more	⇔	less	mehr	⇔	weniger
please	⇔	thank you	bitte	⇔	danke
northwards	⇔	southwards	nordwärts	⇔	südwärts
near	⇔	far	nah	⇔	weit

PAGE 10

without	⇔	with	ohne	⇔	mit

Chapter 5: Cold and Thirsty

thirsty	⇔	hungry	durstig	⇔	hungrig
floor	⇔	ceiling	Fußboden	⇔	(Zimmer-)Decke
special	⇔	ordinary	besonder	⇔	gewöhnlich

PAGE 12

soon	⇔	later	bald	⇔	später

Chapter 6: Warm Food and Drink

PAGE 14

to pull	⇔	to push	ziehen	⇔	schieben
to shout	⇔	to whisper	schreien	⇔	flüstern

Chapter 7: The *Turmoil* Starts Work

PAGE 16

modern	⇔	old-fashioned	modern	⇔	altmodisch

PAGE 17

thin	⇔	thick	dünn	⇔	dick
back	⇔	front	Vorder-	⇔	Hinter-
broken	⇔	mended	kaputt	⇔	ausgebessert, repariert

Chapter 8: A Helper for the Captain

PAGE 18

close to	⇔	far from	nahe	⇔	weit entfernt von
to catch	⇔	to miss	fangen	⇔	nicht fangen

different	⇔	the same	anders	⇔	der/die/dasselbe; der/die/das gleiche
possible	⇔	impossible	möglich	⇔	unmöglich
apart	⇔	together (with)	auseinander	⇔	zusammen (mit)
to smile	⇔	to frown	lächeln	⇔	die Stirn runzeln
life	⇔	death	Leben	⇔	Tod

Chapter 9: Working in the Storm

PAGE 20

dark	⇔	light	dunkel	⇔	hell
sloping	⇔	flat	schräg	⇔	flach
to love	⇔	to hate	lieben	⇔	hassen

PAGE 21

sometimes	⇔	often	manchmal	⇔	oft
once	⇔	twice	einmal	⇔	zweimal

Chapter 10: The Cable Breaks

eastwards	⇔	westwards	ostwärts	⇔	westwärts
before	⇔	after	vor(her)	⇔	nach(her)
in front	⇔	behind	vorne	⇔	hinten
never	⇔	always	nie	⇔	immer

PAGE 22

television	⇔	radio	Fernsehen	⇔	Rundfunk
to agree	⇔	to disagree	zustimmen	⇔	anderer Meinung sein
brave	⇔	cowardly	mutig	⇔	feige
sharp	⇔	blunt; smooth	scharf	⇔	stumpf; glatt
silly	⇔	wise, clever	albern	⇔	weise, klug

Chapter 12: The Ship Sinks

PAGE 27

at the end	⇔	in the middle	am Ende	⇔	in der Mitte
to die	⇔	to live	sterben	⇔	leben
asleep	⇔	awake	eingeschlafen, schlafend	⇔	wach

Vocabulary Page by Page

(See list of short forms on page 35.)

Chapter 1: The Storm Begins

PAGE 3

storm	bad weather, with rain and strong winds	Sturm
Christmas Eve	December 24th; the day before Christmas (Christmas = Weihnachten)	Heiliger Abend
weather	sunshine, wind, rain and snow	Wetter
cold	not warm; like ice or snow	kalt
to blow, blew, blown	The wind *blew* his hat off.	blasen, wehen
ship	big boat that sails on the sea	Schiff
to sail	to travel on the water	segeln, fahren
on the way to	going to (a place)	unterwegs
to carry	1. Mother *carried* the baby into the garden.	tragen
	2. Buses *carry* people to work.	befördern, bringen
cargo	the things that a ship carries	Ladung, Fracht(gut)
crew	people who work on a ship	Besatzung
passenger	person who travels on a ship, a train	Fahrgast, Passagier
to travel	They *travelled* from England to America.	reisen
among	in the middle of; one of ...	(mitten) unter, inmitten
late	You mustn't be *late* for school!; *opp.* early	spät
afternoon	morning – *afternoon* – evening	Nachmittag
dining-room	room where you eat	Speisesaal, -raum
carol	song for Christmas	Weihnachtslied
candle	stick made of wax, which gives light	Kerze
to burn, burnt, burnt	A fire *burns.*	brennen, verbrennen
tree	Apples grow on a *tree.*	Baum
to finish	to end; *opp.* to begin	beenden; fertig sein
captain	the chief person on a ship	Kapitän
very	London is a *very* big city.	sehr
serious	Stop laughing – be *serious!; opp.* funny	ernst
to ask	1. to say that you want (s.o. to do) s.th.	bitten
	2. to try to get an answer	fragen
safe	not hurt, not in danger	sicher, in Sicherheit
during	*During* the night, we sleep.	während
night	*opp.* day	Nacht
slowly	*opp.* quickly	langsam

to get, got, got	1. Close the window – I'm *getting* cold. 2. Children *get* presents on their birthdays.	werden kriegen, bekommen
worse	*Vergleichsform von* bad; *opp.* better	schlimmer
to be worried	to be afraid	s. Sorgen machen
gale	very strong wind	Sturm(wind)
another	one more	noch ein(e)
terrible	No summer holidays – that's *terrible*!	schrecklich
even	She can run fast, but I can run *even* faster.	noch
up	Stand *up*!; *opp.* down	(hin)auf
bows	the front end of a ship	Bug
down	The ball rolled *down* the hill; *opp:* up	(hin)unter
wave	rolling water on the sea	Welle
to batter	to hit hard	gegen etw. schlagen
to toss	to throw about	werfen, schleudern
to and fro	backwards and forwards	hin und her
water	The sea is full of *water.*	Wasser
to splash	to make s.th. wet	*h:* spritzen
deck	floor of a ship	Deck
to roll	The ball *rolled* under the table.	rollen
all night	from evening till morning	die ganze Nacht hindurch
morning	the first part of the day	Morgen, Vormittag
enormous	very, very big	riesig
without	*opp.* with	ohne
suddenly	*Suddenly* the alarm went off.	plötzlich
about	There are *about* thirty children in our class.	*h:* etwa, circa
ear-splitting	very, very loud	ohrenzerreißend
noise	(loud) sound	Lärm; Geräusch
loud	*opp.* quiet	laut

PAGE 4

to crack	to break, but not into pieces; The ball *cracked* the window.	*h:* einen Riss bekommen, aufspringen
middle	centre	Mitte

Chapter 2: The Crack Gets Wider

to hurry	to go (*or* to do s.th.) quickly	eilen; s. beeilen
hold	A ship carries her cargo in the *hold.*	Lade-, Frachtraum
sea-level	how high the sea is	Meereshöhe
sailor	one of the crew on a ship	Matrose
to mend	to repair; Mother *mends* my socks.	ausbessern, flicken; *h:* reparieren
to talk	to speak	reden

quietly	*opp.* loudly	leise
engineer	*h:* person who works with the ship's motors	*h:* Machinist
now	Come here *now!*	jetzt, nun
when	1. *When* he went home, it was raining. 2. *When* did she come? – At three o'clock.	als, wenn wann
question	what you ask	Frage
to happen	The accident *happened* at ten past four.	geschehen, passieren
to think, thought, thought	*Think* before you speak!	denken
over	1. ended; We'll go home when school is *over.* 2. When it rains, you can hold an umbrella *over* your head.	vorüber, vorbei über
to sink, sank sunk	to go down under the water	sinken; versenken
to be drowned	to die under water	ertrinken
to keep calm	to stay quiet, not get excited (to keep = behalten)	ruhig bleiben
to try	to see if you can do s.th.	versuchen; probieren
to repair	to mend	ausbessern; *h:* reparieren
difficult	*opp.* easy	schwierig
early	*opp.* late	früh
cabin	room on a ship	Kabine
since	*Since* last Monday, it has rained every day.	seit
because	My sister is in bed *because* she is ill.	weil
seasick	feeling sick on a boat	seekrank
part	some, but not all	Teil
heavy	I can't carry this bag – it's too *heavy.* *opp.* light	schwer *(von Gewicht)*
steering	This helps you to turn left or right.	Steuer-, Ruderanlage
to steer	to turn a wheel (= Rad) to make a car, bus, ship go left or right	steuern, lenken
to break, broke, broken	*h:* to go wrong and stop working	(zer)brechen; *h:* versagen

PAGE 6

to drift	to be carried along by the water	treiben
helplessly	not able to help yourself	hilflos
real	This is *real* gold, not just yellow metal.	echt
hurricane	great storm with strong winds	Orkan, Sturm
to hit, hit, hit	He cried when she *hit* him.	schlagen (gegen)

to come loose	to become free; (loose = los(e))	s. lösen
to roll about	to move from side to side	herumrollen
to crash	to hit s.th. loudly	krachen, knallen
against	He fell and hit his head *against* the wall.	gegen
to fall over	to fall to the ground (to fall, fell, fallen = fallen)	umfallen
gigantic	very, very big	riesengroß
this time	I walked yesterday; *this time* I'll go by bus.	diesmal
so	My brother has mumps, *so* he isn't at school.	deshalb
to lie, lay, lain	Cathy *lay* on the bed, reading a book.	liegen
tipped	turned on one side	gekippt

Chapter 3: 'SOS! – SOS!'

flat	not going up and down; A table-top is *flat.*	flach
steep	He walked slowly up the *steep* hill.	steil
roof	the top of a house	Dach
to turn	She *turned* round to see who was behind her.	(s.) (um)drehen
radio operator	person who sends radio messages	Funker
already	before now; I've *already* told you that!	schon
to send, sent, sent	Have you *sent* the letter to your uncle?	schicken, senden
message	information that you send to s.o.	Nachricht; *h:* Meldung
important	Milk is *important* for babies.	wichtig, bedeutend
to list	*h:* to lean to one side	*h:* Schlagseite haben
there were	*There were* a lot of children at the party. (there is/there are = es gibt; there will be = es wird geben)	es gab, es waren
as ... as	Thomas is *as* tall *as* the teacher!	so ... wie
to reach	Telephone me when you *reach* London.	erreichen
to have to	must; I *have to* go to school on Monday. (to have = haben)	müssen
to wait (for)	We *waited* at the bus-stop till the bus came.	warten (auf)
but	She is English, *but* she lives in Germany.	aber; sondern
a little	some, but not much	ein wenig
oil	I must put some more *oil* in the car.	Öl

PAGE 7

soon	in a short time; I will come home *soon.*	bald
pool	There were *pools* of water on the road after the storm.	*h:* Lache
to cover	Flood water *covered* the fields.	(zu)decken, bedecken

on board	on the ship	an Bord
everyone	all the people	jeder(mann)
to leave, left, left	to go out of, to go away (from)	verlassen
to use	We *use* a pen to write with.	benutzen
lifeboat	small boat on a ship to save people if the ship sinks (to save = retten)	Rettungsboot
to jump	to spring; The cat *jumped* onto the wall.	springen
lifejacket	This stops you from sinking in the water.	Schwimmweste
together	Paul and I always walk to school *together.*	zusammen
quickly	I finished before you because I write *quickly*.	schnell
to pick up	to take out of the water	*h:* aufnehmen
back and forth	backwards and forwards	hin und her
through	Go *through* that door and turn right!	durch
first ... then	*First* think what to say, *then* say it.	als erstes ... dann
wet	covered with water; *opp.* dry	nass
back	Put the book *back* when you have read it.	zurück
It took a long time.	He walked to school, and *it took* two hours.	Es dauerte lang.
finally	at last; After a long time, they *finally* found the lost child.	schließlich
last	December is the *last* month in the year.	letzte(r, s)
still	I can't go – I'm *still* doing my homework.	(immer) noch
surprised	I'm *surprised* to see you here – I thought you were on holiday.	überrascht
to reply	to answer; "Yes, sir," he *replied*.	antworten; erwidern
alone	After his wife died, he lived *alone*.	allein
someone	a person; *Someone* knocked at the door.	jemand
answer	what you say when a question is asked	Antwort

Chapter 4: Captain Carlsen Alone

to arrive	to come to a place	ankommen
destroyer	a warship	Zerstörer
navy	all the warships of a country	Marine

PAGE 9

to be right	*opp.* to be wrong	recht haben
more and more	We can't go out – it's raining *more and more.*	immer mehr
whole	The *whole* class was quiet – no one spoke.	ganz
loudhailer	thing to make voices (= Stimmen) louder	Lautsprecher

to call	to speak loudly and clearly; to shout	rufen
time	You're lazy – it's *time* you began working hard.	Zeit
thank you	These flowers are for you. – Oh, *thank you!*	danke
to stay	not to go away; On Sundays we *stay* at home.	bleiben
until	till; Wait here *until* I come back.	bis
to tow	to pull a ship, a car	(ab)schleppen
port	town with a place where ships can land	Hafen(stadt)
degree	There are 90 *degrees* in a right angle. (= rechter Winkel)	Grad
no longer	It *no longer* works = It doesn't work any more.	nicht mehr
to fill	*h:* to become full; *opp.* to empty	*h:* s. füllen
meanwhile	Jim ate supper. *Meanwhile* I did my homework.	inzwischen
just	at the moment: We are *just* going out.	gerade, soeben
surprising	S.th. not expected (= unerwartet) is *surprising.*	überraschend
news	report about s.th. that has happened	Nachricht(en)
to order	*h:* to ask s.o. to send s.th.	bestellen; *h:* anfordern
tug	a small ship that tows other ships	Schlepper
to salvage	to save a ship that is sinking	bergen
powerful	strong; able to move heavy things easily	stark, kräftig
world	The Queen is one of the richest people in the *world.*	Welt
only	just; no more than	nur
fresh	I bought *fresh* eggs from the farm.	frisch
supplies	things that people need	Vorräte
to set course for	to go towards	zusteuern auf
shower	a fall of rain or hail	Schauer
hail	rain in the form of ice	Hagel

PAGE 10

sleepless	If you are *sleepless*, then you can't sleep.	schlaflos
hungry	When we are *hungry*, we want to eat s.th.	hungrig
hour	60 minutes	Stunde
Are you all right?	I broke my leg last year, but I'm *all right* now. (all right = in Ordnung)	Geht's Ihnen gut?
to look at	Just *look at* that new car!	anschauen
right	directly; The wind blew *right* in our faces.	*h:* direkt
to hold on	to keep your hand on s.th.; (to hold = halten)	s. festhalten
rope	a strong, thick line	Seil
to wave	to move one's hand or arm	winken
roof	the top of a house	Dach

again	once more; Never do that *again!*	wieder, nochmals

Chapter 5: Cold and Thirsty

floor	part of a room where you stand and walk	Fußboden
wall	the side of a room	Wand
electricity	Washing machines work on *electricity*.	Strom, Elektrizität
especially	She loves all fruit, *especially* bananas.	besonders, vor allem
short-wave	With a *short-wave* radio, you can hear Japan.	Kurzwellen-
kind	sort; What *kind* of music do you like best?	Art
to build, built, built	He is *build*ing a garage next to the house.	bauen
to run, ran, run	to go with fast steps; *h:* to work, to function	laufen
to speak, spoke, spoken	to talk, to say words; She *speaks* very fast.	sprechen
mostly	Cows *mostly* eat grass.	meistens; hauptsächlich
too	1. That question is *too* hard – I can't answer it.	zu (sehr)
	2. Can I come *too?*	auch
special	Johnny is my *special* friend.	besondere(r, s)
please	Will you give me an apple, *please?*	bitte
to tell, told told	to say s.th. to s.o.	erzählen, sagen
wife	*opp.* husband	(Ehe-)Frau

PAGE 12

at any moment	at any time	in jedem Augenblick
might	could perhaps; Don't run – you *might* fall.	könnte (vielleicht)
to seem	That apple is bad, but this one *seems* all right.	scheinen
to have nerves of steel	not to be afraid at all	Nerven wie Drahtseile haben
none	not one	keine(r, s)
light	The sun gives us *light*.	Licht; *h:* Lampe
to work	We can't watch television: it's not *work*ing.	arbeiten; *h:* funktionieren
to look for	to try to find; John is *look*ing for a job.	suchen
to light, lit, lit	to make s.th. start to burn	anzünden
all the time	I don't like him: he talks *all the time*.	die ganze Zeit
far	*opp.* near	weit
to be thirsty	I'*m thirsty* – I must drink something.	Durst haben
hot	*opp.* cold	heiß

to drink, drank, drunk	Babies *drink* milk.	trinken
to boil	to make water hot (=100°C.)	kochen
to do without	There's no sugar, so we'll have to *do without.* (to do = tun, machen)	ohne (etw.) auskommen
to wash	*h:* to move *(water)*	*h:* spülen
to hold on	Can you *hold on* till help comes?	*h:* aushalten, -harren
till	until; We'll wait *till* the rain stops.	bis

Chapter 6: Warm Food and Drink

PAGE 14

food	things you can eat	Speise(n); Essen
drink	Water, milk and coffee are all *drinks.*	Getränk
to go by	to pass; (to go = gehen)	vorübergehen
to eat, ate eaten	He is fat because he *eats* a lot.	essen
let's ...	I think that we should ... (*let's* not .../don't *let's* ... = wollen wir nicht ...)	wollen wir ...
something	There's *something* on the floor – what is it?	etwas
to warm up	to make s.o. or s.th. hot	aufwärmen
gun	You can shoot with this.	Gewehr
in trouble	having problems	*h:* in Not
to shoot, shot, shot	to fire a gun	schießen
across	from one side to the other	(quer) über
to fire	to shoot a gun	feuern, schießen
to fly, flew, flown	to go through the air	fliegen
to catch, caught, caught	Try and *catch* this ball!	fangen
to slope	A hill *slopes.*	abschüssig sein
hard	difficult; *opp.* easy	schwierig
to scramble	to walk *or* climb with difficulty	krabbeln, klettern
to miss	*h:* not to catch	*h:* nicht fangen
second	1, 2, 3, 4 – first, *second*, third, fourth	zweite(r, s)
third	1, 2, 3, 4 – first, second, *third*, fourth	dritte(r, s)
fourth	1, 2, 3, 4 – first, second, third, *fourth*	vierte(r, s)
to tie	to make a knot	binden, festmachen
rail	Round the deck there is a *rail.*	Geländer, Reling

box	He gave his wife a *box* of chocolates.	Schachtel; Kiste
to hang, hung, hung	She *hung* the washing on the line to dry.	(auf)hängen
to swing, swung, swung	The monkey was *swing*ing from the tree.	pendeln, schaukeln, baumeln
to pull	to move s.th. towards you; *opp.* to push	ziehen
at last	in the end, finally	schließlich; endlich
to shout	*opp.* to speak quietly	schreien
cap	a sort of soft hat	Mütze
thanks	He went out, without a word of *thanks.*	Dank
along	from one end towards the other	entlang

PAGE 16

coffee	Two cups of tea and a black *coffee*, please!	Kaffee
week	seven days (weak = schwach!)	Woche
sweets	Chocolates and toffees are *sweets.*	Bonbons, Süßigkeiten
magazine	thin book with a paper cover which comes out every week, month	Zeitschrift
to gaze at	to look at s.th. for a long time	lange betrachten
to feel, felt, felt	Could we open the window, please? I *feel* hot. (= Mir ist heiß.)	(s.) fühlen
meal	Breakfast, lunch and dinner are *meals.*	Mahlzeit
funnel	the chimney of a ship	Schornstein *(vom Schiff)*
nearly	almost; Let's go home – it's *nearly* lunchtime.	fast, beinahe
to hope	to wish that s.th. will happen	hoffen

Chapter 7: The *Turmoil* Starts Work

to cheer	to shout "hurray!"	"hurra!" rufen
evening	morning – afternoon – *evening*	Abend
tired	The *tired* boy fell asleep quickly.	müde, ermüdet
happy	*opp.* sad	glücklich
to die down	to become weaker	nachlassen
so that	Speaker louder *so that* I can hear you!	damit
small	little	klein
engine	motor	Triebwerk, Motor
immense	very, very big	ungeheuer, riesig
equipment	things to do a job with	Ausrüstung
immediately	at once; I can't wait – we must go *immediately.*	sofort
dark	At night it is *dark. opp.* light	dunkel
of course	naturally	natürlich

PAGE 17

easy	I did the homework quickly because it was *easy*. (= simple); *opp.* difficult	leicht
thin	not thick; not fat	dünn
weak	*opp.* strong; (w*ee*k = Woche!)	schwach
thick	*opp.* thin	dick, stark
steel	strong hard metal for knives, machines (to st*ea*l = stehlen!)	Stahl
cable	a strong, thick rope	Kabel
both	two together	beide
overboard	over the side of the boat and into the water	über Bord
low	not high	*h:* tief
stern	the back end of a ship	Heck
rudder	thing at the back of a ship to make it turn	Steuerruder
above	over	über
whose	of whom; of which (who's = who is!)	dessen, deren; wessen
to need	We *need* water to live.	brauchen, benötigen
help	The walking-stick was a big *help* to the old man.	Hilfe
to fix	to put s.th. in place so that it won't move	*h:* festmachen
between	Sit here in the middle – *between* us!	zwischen

Chapter 8: A Helper for the Captain

twice	two times	zweimal
to move	to go from one place to another	s. bewegen

PAGE 18

close to	(very) near to	nahe, dicht
to look	*h:* to seem to be: You *look* very happy today.	aussehen
tiny	very, very small	winzig
to aim	to point a gun at s.th.	zielen
the same	*opp.* different	der/die/dasselbe; der/die/das gleiche
by himself	alone →wie alleine	allein, ohne Hilfe
impossible	It is *impossible* for elephants to fly!	unmöglich
to lift up	to take s.th. up	aufheben
to bump	to hit against s.th.	stoßen, prallen (gegen)
to grab	to take s.th. quickly with your hand	(hastig) greifen, packen
second	There are 60 *seconds* in a minute.	Sekunde
apart	The two houses are 500 metres *apart*.	auseinander
to climb	to go up with hands and feet	steigen

to land	to come onto the ground	landen
to smile	to have a happy look on your face	lächeln
to risk	to put s.th. in danger (danger = Gefahr)	aufs Spiel setzen
life (*pl.* lives)	The old man lost his *life* in the fire.	Leben
to shake hands (with)	to give your hand to s.o. when you meet him (to shake = schütteln)	(jmd.) die Hand geben

Chapter 9: Working in the Storm

PAGE 20

fog	thick cloud (= Wolke) on the ground that stops you seeing clearly	Nebel
to close in	*h:* to come in near to	*h:* umschließen
again and again	many times	immer wieder
to slip off	to fall off	hinunterrutschen
once	one time	einmal
to manage to	to be able to (do s.th. difficult)	es schaffen, etw. zu tun
to crash	*h:* to fall hard	*h:* hereinbrechen über
hammock	bed that you hang up on a ship	Hängematte
cake	We had tea and *cakes* at five o'clock.	Kuchen
to light up	*h:* to look very happy	*h:* aufleuchten
I'm sorry.	1. *I'm sorry* that your father has died. 2. *I'm sorry* – I've forgotten my homework.	Es tut mir leid ...; leider
except	but not: He works every day *except* Sunday.	außer
to clear	*h:* to go away	*h:* s. auflösen
as soon as	He went home *as soon as* school was over.	sobald
light	It is *light* in the daytime, and dark at night.	hell

PAGE 21

sometimes	from time to time	manchmal
weight	how heavy s.th. is	Gewicht
to fasten	to fix s.th. so that it can't move	festmachen
to bleed, bled, bled	to lose blood (= Blut)	bluten
tight	*h:* pulled so that it is straight	*h:* straff, gespannt

Chapter 10: The Cable Breaks

normally	mostly; usually	normalerweise
to walk	to go on foot, but not run	spazierengehen, laufen
anyway	It's raining, but we're going for a walk *anyway*.	jedenfalls, sowieso
several	some, but not many	einige
to pass	to go by	vorübergehen

while	The mothers talked *while* the children played.	während
to continue	to go on doing s.th.	fortfahren; s. fortsetzen
at least	If you forget your homework, *at least* you should say 'sorry'!	wenigstens

PAGE 22

helicopter	a sort of small plane with a rotor on top	Hubschrauber
newspaper	The 'Daily Mirror' is an English *newspaper*. (See the title page on the cover of this book!)	Zeitung
reporter	person who writes stories for a newspaper	Journalist(in)
proud of	pleased about s.th. that s.o. has done	stolz auf
to circle	to go round; to move in a circle (= Kreis)	kreisen
photograph	picture that you take with a camera (to take photos = Fotos machen)	Foto
later	afterwards, after this time	später
plane	machine that can fly	Flugzeug
to listen to	to hear carefully; to try to hear	zuhören; horchen
to discuss	to talk about s.th.	besprechen; diskutieren
to agree	to think the same; to have the same ideas	übereinstimmen
really	I had no breakfast this morning – now I'm *really* hungry!	wirklich
brave	She was not afraid; it was *brave* of her to go into the burning house.	mutig
ever	Have you *ever* been to England?	je(mals)
to rise, rose, risen	to become higher	(an)steigen; aufgehen *(Sonne)*
accident	Two people were killed in a car *accident*.	Unfall
every two hours	Take these pills *every two hours!* (every = jede(r, s))	alle zwei Stunden
to smear	to spread soft stuff on s.th.	schmieren
a bit	a little; Let's stop – I'm *a bit* tired.	ein bisschen; ein wenig
silly	foolish, stupid	dumm, albern

PAGE 24

to dry	to make s.th. dry	trocknen
clothes	pullovers, T-shirts, socks	Kleider
We're making good progress.	Things are going well. (progress = Fortschritt(e))	Wir kommen gut voran.
medal	In the Olympic Games, the winner gets a gold *medal*.	Orden; Medaille
to head for	to go towards	Kurs halten auf

away from	from there	von ... entfernt
a while	a (short) time	eine Weile
weather report	The *weather report* says it will rain tomorrow.	Wetterbericht

Chapter 11: The Storm Gets Worse

PAGE 25

ceiling	part of a room over our heads	(Zimmer-)Decke
almost	nearly; Don't go – dinner is *almost* ready.	fast, beinahe

Chapter 12: The Ship Sinks

both ... and	We are learning *both* English *and* French.	sowohl ... als auch
to abandon	to leave for ever	aufgeben; verlassen
to beat, beat, beaten	to hit hard, again and again	schlagen
to dip	Paul *dipped* his spoon into the soup.	(ein)tauchen

PAGE 27

to follow	to go after (s.o. or s.th.)	folgen
bad luck	I have lost my watch. – Oh, *bad luck!*	Pech
crowd	big group of people	(Menschen-)Menge
horn	thing in a car or ship to make warning sounds	Hupe; Signalhorn
siren	This makes a long, loud noise to warn people.	Sirene
to sound	*h:* to make a noise	ertönen, erschallen
fast asleep	deep in sleep	tief im Schlaf

Exercises

Some Ideas for Working on these Exercises

The following exercises offer over 650 questions: a wide variety which the teacher can choose from to suit the needs of different classes.

- ✧ *This may well be pupils' first experience of working from printed exercises. In this case, it is important to introduce the different exercise types orally in class, practising until a certain degree of familiarity is achieved before setting questions as homework.*
- ✧ *In class, pupils can work all together, individually or in small groups of two to four. The work can be done spontaneously in class, prepared in class or prepared at home. Homework can be written out normally for the teacher or prepared in draft form for oral work in class.*
- ✧ *The class could divide themselves and an exercise into three parts and do, for example, questions 1–3, questions 4–6 and questions 7–9. Preparation time is thus reduced, though pupils are still exposed to the full range of material through the others' contributions.*
- ✧ *Different groups of the class can work on different exercises. If it seems useful, assignments could then be switched/rotated for the following homework or practice sessions. Thus*

Monday:	*Group 1 – Exercise 1;*	*Group 2 – Exercise 2;*
Tuesday:	*Group 1 – Exercise 3;*	*Group 2 – Exercise 4;*

  would emphasise variety and fast progress, while

Monday:	*Group 1 – Exercise 1;*	*Group 2 – Exercise 2;*
Tuesday:	*Group 1 – Exercise 2;*	*Group 2 – Exercise 1;*

  would provide more thoroughness at a slower pace while still retaining some variety in the lesson itself. This, of course, can be done just as well with three or four groups, and also while using only parts of each exercise.
- ✧ *When the class is well into the text and all the main types of exercise have been worked on, some groups may enjoy the following: Each child chooses (freely, or with guidance from the teacher) a particular exercise from the repertoire of those already worked on. This exercise must be so prepared that answers can be given orally without looking at the text or printed exercise. The questions can be asked – in or out of order – by the class and/or teacher.*
- ✧ *Happy Learning!*

Exercise 1— What (page 3) — CHAPTER 1

1. What was sailing from Hamburg to New York?
2. What was the ship carrying?
3. What were the passengers in the dining-room singing?
4. What was burning on the Christmas tree?
5. What had the passengers just finished?
6. What did one of the crew give the captain?
7. What got slowly worse?
8. What battered the sides of the ship?
9. What splashed over her decks?
10. What was even louder than the noise of the storm?

Exercise 2 — Who (pages 3–4)

1. Who was on the ship?
2. Who was in the dining-room, singing?
3. Who came in when they had finished *Silent Night, Holy Night*?
4. Who became very serious?
5. Who should go to their cabins?
6. Who was worried?
7. Who said that this wasn't just a strong wind?
8. Who came running to the captain?

Exercise 3 — When and Where (pages 3–4)

1. When did the story begin?
2. Where was the ship when the story began?
3. Where was the ship sailing from?
4. Where was the ship sailing to?
5. When were the passengers in the dining-room?
6. When did one of the crew come in?
7. When did the weather slowly get worse?
8. Where did water splash, as the ship rolled from side to side?
9. When did the wind blow harder?
10. When was it a terrible storm?
11. When was there an ear-splitting noise?
12. Where has the ship cracked?

Exercise 4 — Short Answers (pages 4–6)

1. Did the captain hurry down to the hold?
2. Did he want to see the crack?
3. Did it go across the deck and down the sides?
4. Did the captain talk quietly to the first engineer?
5. Did some passengers run to the captain with questions?
6. Did the captain ask the passengers questions?
7. Did the captain say, "The ship's going to sink"?
8. Did the captain say, "We must all keep calm"?
9. Did the storm go on and on?
10. Did the crack begin to open wider and wider?

Exercise 5 — Either/Or (pages 4–6)

1. Were the sailors on the deck or down in the hold?
2. Were they working hard or were they sleeping?
3. Was the job easy or difficult?
4. Was it now the morning or the evening of December 27th?
5. Had the passengers been in their cabins or in the hold?

6. Were the passengers happy or terribly seasick?
7. Can the crew steer the ship, or is she drifting?
8. Was the storm just a strong wind, or was it a real hurricane?
9. Did the passengers fall on the deck or into the water?
10. Was the ship now sailing normally, or was she tipped to one side?

Exercise 6 — Describing a Picture (page 5)

1. What can you see in the picture on page 5?
   Write at least four sentences.

Exercise 7 — Vocabulary (pages 3–6)

1. What is the name for *December 24th?*
2. What is a word for *very, very cold?*
3. What do we call the *goods which a ship is carrying?*
4. What is the word for the *people who work on a ship?*
5 What is the word for a *song for Christmas?*
6. What is the name for the *chief person on a ship?*
7. What do we call a *room on a ship?*
8. What is the opposite of *quickly?*
9. What is the opposite of *better?*
10. What do we call the *sharp end of a ship?*
11. What is the opposite of *down?*
12. What is the opposite of *last* week?
13. What is a word meaning *very, very big?*
14. What is the word for *to go or do something quickly?*
15. What is the opposite of *loudly?*
16. What is one word for *afraid that something is wrong?*
17. What is the opposite of *answers?*
18. What is the opposite of *easy?*
19. What is the opposite of *to close?*
20. What is one word for a *very big sea?*

Exercise 8 — Did You Understand Chapters 1 & 2? (pages 3–6)

1. Where does the story begin?
2. What was the weather like?
3. Who was on board the ship?
4. What was the piece of paper that one of the crew gave the captain?
5. What happened during the night?
6. What was the storm like, the next morning?
7. What happened at 2 o'clock in the afternoon?
8. What did the captain do when he heard about the crack?
9. Who did he talk to?

10. What were three of the questions the passengers asked the captain?
11. Can the sailors mend the crack?
12. Why couldn't the passengers eat anything?
13. What happened when the weather grew even worse?
14. Why couldn't the ship roll back after the gigantic wave had hit her?
15. How did the ship lie in the water now?

Exercise 9 — Who (pages 6–7) **CHAPTER 3**

1. Who sent out the SOS message?
2. Who spoke to all the people on board?
3. Who must leave the ship now?
4. Who put on their life-jackets?
5. Who jumped together with the first passengers?
6. Who did the motorboats take to the other ships?
7. Who did the boats pick up finally, at ten past five?
8. Who is still on the *Flying Enterprise*?
9. Who looked over the stormy sea?
10. Who was standing alone on the deck?

Exercise 10 — Put into the Past Tense (pages 6–7)

1. There *are* three other ships in this part of the Atlantic.
2. When they *hear* the SOS message, they *turn* and *sail* towards Captain Carlsen's ship.
3. The captain *tells* all the people on board to leave the ship.
4. The first passengers *jump* into the stormy sea.
5. The water *is* like ice.
6. Motorboats from the other ships *are* waiting.
7. The wind *blows* as the boats *go* back and forth.
8. First they *take* the cold, wet people to the other ships.
9. Then they *wait* to pick up the next people.
10. Finally they *pick* up the last of the crew.
11. The sailors and crew *look* over the stormy sea at the ship.
12. Captain Carlsen *is* standing alone on the deck.

Exercise 11 — Short Answers (pages 6–7)

1. Is the deck flat?
2. Did the radio operator send out an SOS message?
3. Is the message from the *Flying Enterprise?*
4. Is water coming into the hold?
5. Is the ship listing to one side?
6. Is the ship sinking?

7. Did other ships hear the SOS message?
8. Did the captain say, "Everyone must leave the ship now"?
9. Did they use the ship's lifeboats?
10. Did they all put on their lifejackets?
11. Did the passengers jump into the sea?
12. Did the motorboats come from the other ships?

Exercise 12 — Opposites (pages 6–7)

1. What is the opposite of *to sit down?*
2. What is the opposite of *far away?*
3. What is the opposite of *to swim?*
4. What is the opposite of *away from?*
5. What is the opposite of *everything?*
6. What is the opposite of *to stop* or *to finish?*
7. What is the opposite of *nobody?*
8. What is the opposite of *to take off?*
9. What is the opposite of *to answer?*
10. What is the opposite of *together* or *with other people?*

Exercise 13 — Describing a Picture (page 8)

1. What can you see in the picture on page 8? Write at least five sentences.

Exercise 14 — What (pages 7–9)

1. What were the waves still battering?
2. What new ship arrived now?
3. What did the *Willard Keith's* captain take, to call Captain Carlsen?
4. What no longer worked?
5. What was slowly filling with water?
6. What day of the week was January 1st, 1952?
7. What had the American sailors heard?
8. What was the *Turmoil?*
9. What did the *Turmoil* pick up in Falmouth?
10. What was the weather like, when the *Turmoil* left port?

Exercise 15 — Where (pages 7–10)

1. Where was Captain Carlsen?
2. Where were the waves breaking?
3. Where were the American sailors?
4. Where will Captain Carlsen stay?
5. Where did the *Flying Enterprise* drift?
6. Where was the *Willard Keith* sailing on January 1st?

7. Where was the *Turmoil* when Captain Carlsen ordered a tug?
8. Where was the port of Falmouth?
9. Where did the *Turmoil* pick up supplies?
10. Where had Captain Carlsen been for five days now?

Exercise 16 — Put into the Past Tense (page 9)

1. The ship *drifts* northwards on the stormy sea.
2. She *is* leaning sixty degrees to the side.
3. Her steering no longer *works*.
4. Now it *is* January 1st, 1952.
5. The American destroyer *is* sailing as near to the ship as she *can*.
6. The American sailors *are* very surprised.
7. The tug *is* the most powerful one in the world.
8. But at this time she *isn't* in port.
9. She *is* towing another ship across the Bay of Biscay.
10. On January 2nd, the tug *arrives* at Falmouth.
11. She *turns* round after only twenty minutes.
12. Then she *sails* for the North Atlantic.

Exercise 17 — Short Answers (pages 9–10)

1. Was January 1st, 1952, a Tuesday?
2. Was the *Willard Keith* sailing near to the *Flying Enterprise?*
3. Did Captain Carlsen think he could save his ship?
4. Did he order a tug to salvage the *Flying Enterprise?*
5. Was the *Turmoil* a destroyer?
6. Was the *Turmoil* in port at this time?
7. Did the *Turmoil* arrive at Falmouth the next day?
8. Did she wait at Falmouth for twenty days?
9. Was Captain Carlsen alone on his ship?
10. Was the captain sleepless and hungry?
11. Did the waves break right over the ship?
12. Did Captain Carlsen wave with both hands?
13. Did Captain Carlsen roll off the ship and into the sea?
14. Did he go into one of the cabins?

Exercise 18 — Vocabulary (pages 7–10)

1. What is another word for *to come to a place?*
2. What is a word meaning *very bad, dreadful, awful?*
3. What is one word for *in a short time?*
4. What is a word for ships meaning *to lean a lot to one side?*
5. What is the name for a *small machine to make your voice louder?*

6. What do we call a *town by the sea where ships can land?*
7. What is the opposite of *far?*
8. How do we describe something *that we don't expect?*
9. What is a word meaning *to save a ship which is sinking?*
10. What is another word for *very strong?*
11. What is a word for *things that people need, especially food and drink?*
12. What is the word in the text for *rain in the form of ice?*
13. What is the opposite of *dry?*
14. What is a 'pair word' for *thirsty?*
15. What is the opposite of *to put down?*
16. What do we call *rolling water on the sea?*
17. What is the word for *a very thick, strong line?*
18. What is the opposite of *with?*
19. What is the opposite of *to stand?*
20. What is a word meaning *to go under the water?*

Exercise 19 — Describing a Picture (page 11)

1. What can you see in the picture on page 11? Write at least five sentences.

Exercise 20 — Did You Understand Chapters 3 & 4? (pages 6–10)

1. Why can't the passengers stand up?
2. What is the radio operator's message?
3. What did the other ships do when they heard the SOS?
4. Why can't the passengers use the ship's lifeboats?
5. How did the passengers and crew leave the ship?
6. What did the motorboats from the other ships do?
7. Where was Captain Carlsen standing?
8. What was the sea like when the *Willard Keith* arrived?
9. What do the American sailors think?
10. What does the *Willard Keith's* captain say to Captain Carlsen?
11. What does Captain Carlsen plan to do?
12. What is the news which surprises the American sailors?
13. Why can't the *Turmoil* leave port before January 2nd?
14. What was Captain Carlsen's situation like, alone on the *Flying Enterprise?*
15. Why was Captain Carlsen holding onto a rope on the deck?

Exercise 21 — Who/What (pages 10–12) **CHAPTER 5**

1. What was listing very badly now?
2. Who had to stand on the wall of his cabin?

3. What did Captain Carlsen have in his cabin?
4. What did he send to the American destroyer?
5. Who was the message for?
6. What will be here soon?
7. What grew stronger when night fell?
8. What did the captain look for?
9. What couldn't he make, because he had no hot water?
10. What did he drink?

Exercise 22 — Put into the Past Tense (page 12)

1. Night *falls*, and the wind *grows* stronger.
2. Big waves *begin* to batter the ship again.
3. Captain Carlsen's ship *drifts* helplessly on the sea.
4. None of the lights *work* now.
5. So the captain *looks* for a candle.
6. Finally, he *finds* one and *lights* it.
7. All the time, the ship *is* going up and down in the storm.
8. The captain *doesn't* sleep much.
9. He *can't* sleep because he *has* to watch the ship.
10. He *is* cold and thirsty.
11. Without electricity, he *can't* make tea.
12. He *finds* some lemonade and *drinks* it slowly.

Exercise 23 — Either/Or (pages 10–12)

1. Was Captain Carlsen on deck or in his cabin?
2. Did he stand on the floor of his cabin or on the wall?
3. Was there electricity or no electricity on the *Flying Enterprise* now?
4. Was the captain's message for his wife or for the *Turmoil?*
5. Is the *Turmoil* on her way now, or is she still in Falmouth?
6. Did the captain turn the lights on, or did he light a candle?
7. Could the captain sleep, or did he have to watch the ship?
8. Did he want some hot tea, or did he want lemonade?
9. Did he drink hot tea, or did he drink cold lemonade?
10. Can Captain Carlsen hold on, or does he want to leave his ship?

Exercise 24 — Opposites (pages 10–12)

1. What is the opposite of *without?*
2. What is the opposite of *good?*
3. What is the opposite of *a question?*

4. What is the opposite of *slowly?*
5. What is the opposite of *day?*
6. What is the opposite of *weak?*
7. What is the opposite of *empty?*
8. What is the opposite of *tiny, very small?*
9. What is the opposite of *near?*
10. What is a 'pair word' for *hungry?*
11. What is the opposite of *hot?*
12. What is a 'pair word' for *to eat?*
13. What is the opposite of *to come?*
14. What is the opposite of *short?*
15. What is the opposite of *to leave, to go away?*

Exercise 25 — Describing a Picture (page 13)

1. What can you see in the picture on page 13?
   Write at least five sentences.

Exercise 26 — Short Answers (pages 14) **CHAPTER 6**

1. Was the sea still stormy?
2. Was the weather hot?
3. Did Captain Carlsen have anything hot to eat?
4. Could the destroyer get near the *Flying Enterprise?*
5. Did the sailors on the destroyer have a special gun?
6. Did the sailors fire the gun?
7. Did they want to sink the *Flying Enterprise?*
8. Did the rope fall on the deck of the *Flying Enterprise?*
9. Was it easy for Captain Carlsen to scramble along
   the deck?
10. Did Captain Carlsen miss the rope?
11. Did the rope fall into the sea?
12. Did Captain Carlsen catch the second and third ropes?

Exercise 27 — Put into the Past Tense (page 14)

1. On the destroyer the sailors *have* a special gun.
2. This gun *can* shoot a rope across to another ship.
3. The sailors *go* to the gun and *fire* it.
4. The rope *flies* across the water.
5. It *falls* on the deck of Captain Carlsen's ship.
6. Captain Carlsen *tries* to catch the rope.
7. But the ship *is* listing too much.
8. So the sailors on the destroyer *have* to try again.
9. Finally, Captain Carlsen *catches* the rope.

10. He *ties* it to a rail.
11. Now the sailors *hang* a box on the rope.
12. Captain Carlsen *pulls* the box slowly towards him.

Exercise 28— Who/What (page 14)

1. What was icy?
2. Who had nothing hot to eat or drink?
3. Who couldn't get near the *Flying Enterprise*?
4. What did the sailors have on board the destroyer?
5. What did the special gun shoot?
6. Who fired the gun?
7. What did the rope fall on?
8. Who missed the rope?
9. What did Captain Carlsen tie the next rope to?
10. What did the sailors tie to the rope?

Exercise 29 — Describing a Picture (page 15)

Up to now, you have probably made short sentences when describing pictures, perhaps like: "I can see Captain Carlsen" or "In the picture I can see the cabin". For this exercise, you should make longer sentences. Instead of just naming a person or thing, say something about them too. Try to make up three different parts after the "I can see ..."

Examples:	*I can see*	①*the captain*	②*hurry**ing***	③*down to the hold.*
	I can see	①*the sailors*	②*mend**ing***	③*the crack.*
	I can see	①*the captain*	②*talk**ing***	③*to the first engineer.*

1. What can you see in the picture on page 15?
   Write at least five longer sentences.

Exercise 30 — Vocabulary (pages 14–16)

1. What is the word for *60 minutes?*
2. What is the name for *the day before Friday?*
3. What do we call *the month after December?*
4. What is the opposite of *something* or *everything?*
5. What is a word for *the things that you eat?*
6. What do we call a *thing that you can shoot with?*
7. What is the opposite of *easy*?
8. What is a word meaning *not to catch* something?
9. What is a word meaning *to make a knot, to bind* s.th. to something else?
10. What do we call *something made of wood or metal, that you can put things in?*
11. What is another way to say *finally?*
12. What word do you shout when you are very pleased about something?

13. What is the opposite of *to whisper?*
14. What is a word meaning *to look at something for a long time?*
15. What is the word for the *chimney of a ship?*

Exercise 31 — Did You Understand Chapters 5 & 6? (pages 10–16)

1. Why couldn't Captain Carlsen stand on the floor of his cabin?
2. What was Captain Carlsen's message to his wife?
3. What happened when night fell?
4. Why did the captain look for a candle?
5. Why didn't the captain sleep much?
6. Why couldn't Captain Carlsen make any hot tea?
7. How far was the ship from England?
8. How could the destroyer's special gun help ships in trouble?
9. Why couldn't Captain Carlsen catch the first rope?
10. What did he do with the fourth rope?
11. How did the box get from the *Willard Keith* to the *Flying Enterprise?*
12. What did the captain do after he had caught the box?
13. What was in the box?
14. What was the problem with the *Flying Enterprise's* funnel?
15. What is the only hope for the *Flying Enterprise?*

Exercise 32 — Short Answers (pages 16–17) **CHAPTER 7**

1. Did the sailors all cheer?
2. Was Captain Carlsen wet and tired?
3. Had the wind died down in the afternoon?
4. Was the rain heavier now?
5. Did they have to get a rope to the *Flying Enterprise*?
6. Was the *Turmoil* American?
7. Were her engines immensely strong?
8. Was it easy to shoot a rope over to Captain Carlsen's ship?
9. Was this rope strong enough to tow the ship?
10. Would Captain Carlsen have to pull the cable onto his ship?

Exercise 33 — Either/Or (pages 16–17)

1. Was the *Turmoil* English or American?
2. Was she bigger than the other ships or smaller?
3. Did the crew begin work in the morning or in the evening?
4. Would they tow the ship with a thin rope or with a heavy cable?

5. Would Captain Carlsen pull the cable with one hand or with both hands?
6. Is it going to be easy or hard for the captain, alone?
7. Does Captain Carlsen need help, or can he do it alone?
8. Is Captain Carlsen holding onto the rails or is he waving?

Exercise 34 – Put into the Future Tense (pages 16–17)

*Example: The Turmoil **helped** the Flying Enterprise.* ⇨
*The Turmoil **will help** the Flying Enterprise.*

1. The tug *arrived* on Thursday evening.
2. Captain Carlsen *was* very happy.
3. The crew of the tug *began* work immediately.
4. They *shot* a rope over to Captain Carlsen's ship.
5. The captain *tried* to catch the rope.
6. But he *needed* help.
7. The tug *sailed* nearer to the big ship..

Exercise 35 – Who/What (page 17)

1. What would the crew have to tie to the first rope?
2. What would they tie to the thicker rope?
3. Who would have to pull the cable onto his ship?
4. What was listing badly?
5. Who would fall overboard if he worked with both hands?
6. Who could see that the ship was low in the water?
7. What was above the waves, at the stern of the ship?
8. Who was the mate of the *Turmoil*?
9. Who is holding onto the ship's rails?
10. What have they got to fix between the ship and the tug?

Exercise 36 – Short Answers (pages 17–18)

1. Did the crew try to get a rope to Captain Carlsen?
2. Was it Friday evening when they began again?
3. Did they try first at the front end of the ship?
4. Was the funnel close to the water now?
5. Did a man on the tug fire the rope-gun?
6. Could Captain Carlsen catch the rope with one hand?
7. Did Mr Dancy jump and grab the rail of the ship?
8. Did he fall into the sea?
9. Was Captain Carlsen's first name Kenneth?
10. Was it Kurt?

Exercise 37 — Either/Or (page 18)

1. Did Captain Carlsen catch the ropes from the *Turmoil*, or did he miss them?
2. Was the tug near the ship or far away?
3. Did the tug bump against the destroyer or against the *Flying Enterprise*?
4. Did Mr Dancy jump over to the ship or into the water?
5. Did he grab the rail of the *Turmoil* or of the *Flying Enterprise*?
6. Did Mr Dancy climb up the stern or the bows?
7. Did he scramble up the deck or back to the *Turmoil*?
8. Was Mr Dancy's name Kurt or Kenneth?

Exercise 38 — Vocabulary (pages 16–18)

1. What is the opposite of *late*?
2. What are *the bows* of a ship?
3. What do we call the *back end of a ship*?
4. What is another word for *nearly*?
5. What is another word for *to shoot* a gun?
6. What is the opposite of *different*?
7. Captain Carlsen is *alone* = Captain Carlsen is ... .
8. If something *can never happen*, then it is ....
9. What is the word for *two together*?
10. Sixty ... make a minute.
11. When you meet someone for the first time, you say your name and then ....
12. If you are ..., you need sleep.
13. What is the word for *to have a happy look on your face*?
14. How do we say *to give someone your hand when you meet him*?

Exercise 39 — Describing a Picture (page 19)

1. What can you see in the picture on page 19? Write at least five longer sentences, as in Exercise 29.

Exercise 40 — Did You Understand Chapters 7 & 8? (pages 16–18)

1. Why do the sailors on the destroyer all cheer?
2. How did Captain Carlsen feel after his days alone?
3. Why did they have to get a rope to the *Flying Enterprise*?
4. How could the *Turmoil* tow the *Flying Enterprise* when she was so much smaller?
5. How could the tug shoot a rope over to the ship?
6. Why did Captain Carlsen have only one hand to pull the cable with?

7. Why will it be hard to fix a cable between the ships?
8. What happened when the *Turmoil* bumped against the *Flying Enterprise*?
9. How did Mr Dancy get on board the big ship?
10. How did the two men greet each other?
11. How had Mr Dancy risked his life?
12. Why did he risk his life?

Exercise 41 — Short Answers (page 20)

1. Were there two men on the ship now?
2. Was it Friday morning?
3. Did the tug fire a rope again and again?
4. Could the men reach these ropes?
5. Did they manage to catch the rope once?
6. Did Mr Dancy take the rope into the cabin?
7. Did the men go into the cabin when it was dark?
8. Was the captain's hammock on the deck?
9. Was there some cake in the hammock?
10. Did Mr Dancy like cake?
11. Can the men hang up a hammock for Mr Dancy?
12. Must Mr Dancy wear a lifejacket?

Exercise 42 — Put into the Present Tense (page 20)

1. It *was* January 4th.
2. Now there *were* two men on the ship.
3. Again and again, the tug *fired* a rope over to the ship.
4. But the rope always *fell* into the water.
5. Once, they *managed* to catch the rope.
6. They *tried* to tie it to the stern.
7. But the ship *was* shaking so much that the rope slipped off.
8. All the time, waves *came* crashing onto the ship.
9. Water *washed* around them on the decks.
10. Finally, it *grew* dark.

Exercise 43 — Either/Or (pages 20–21)

1. Was there a piece of cake or a sandwich in the hammock?
2. Does Mr Dancy like cake or does he hate it?
3. Will the men hang up a hammock on the deck or in the cabin?
4. Must Mr Dancy wear a swimming costume or a lifejacket?
5. Did Mr Dancy take the lifejacket off or did he put it on?
6. Did the two men eat cake or bread and cheese?

7. Was the ship sailing to America or was she drifting in heavy seas?
8. Was the weather better in the morning, or worse?
9. Did the men fix the cable in the morning or in the evening?
10. Was the tug towing the ship, or was the *Flying Enterprise* sailing along by herself?

Exercise 44 — Mixed Questions (pages 20–21)

1. Who put on the lifejacket?
2. When did the two men sit and talk?
3. What did they both eat?
4. Where was the funnel now?
5. When did the tug try again to shoot a rope?
6. Where did the tug try to shoot the rope?
7. What was too heavy for the two men?
8. When did they finally manage to pull the cable onto the ship?
9. Where did they fasten the cable?
10. Who cheered when the men had fastened the cable?

Exercise 45 — Did You Understand Chapter 9? (pages 20–21)

1. What happened again and again to the rope that the tug fired?
2. What did the men do with the rope that they managed to catch?
3. Why did this rope, too, slip off into the water?
4. What did the men do when it grew dark?
5. Why did Mr Dancy's eyes light up?
6. Why did Captain Carlsen give Mr Dancy a lifejacket?
7. What did the men do in the evening?
8. Why did the men let the steel cable go, the next day?
9. What new thing happened, that Saturday morning?
10. Why did the tug begin to sail away?

Exercise 46 — Mixed Questions (page 21) **CHAPTER 10**

1. Which ship sailed in front?
2. Where was the *Flying Enterprise*?
3. Where did the *Willard Keith* sail?
4. When is the weather never good, in the North Atlantic?
5. What did the destroyer sometimes do?
6. Who could send a box to the other ship?
7. Where were the sailors?
8. How could the sailors send the box?
9. Who did they send the box to?
10. What was in the box?
11. Where were the two men?

Exercise 47 — Mixed Questions (page 22)

1. What flew out from England?
2. Who was the helicopter carrying?
3. Where did the helicopter fly out from?
4. Who was from England and from Denmark?
5. Who came from Copenhagen?
6. Who was very proud of Captain Carlsen?
7. Where did the helicopter circle?
8. Who took photographs?
9. What came over later?
10. How did water get into the *Flying Enterprise?*

Exercise 48 — Put into the Present Tense (pages 21–22)

1. The *Willard Keith* sailed along beside the other ships.
2. Sometimes she shot a rope over to the *Flying Enterprise.*
3. This was easier now, because the weather was better. *(Two verbs!)*
4. With this rope, the sailors could send supplies to the two men.
5. A helicopter flew out from England.
6. The newspaper photographers were from England and Denmark.
7. They took photographs of the ship from the helicopter.
8. All the time, water was slowly filling the ship.
9. Newspapers were full of stories about the *Flying Enterprise.*
10. Everyone said that Captain Carlsen was very brave. *(Two verbs!)*

Exercise 49 — Short Answers (page 22)

1. Did many people have television in those days?
2. Did millions of people listen to the radio?
3. Was there a lot of talk on the radio about the *Flying Enterprise?*
4. Did people think the two men were very brave?
5. Was the weather in the Atlantic getting worse again now?
6. Did the wind grow stronger?
7. Did the waves rise higher?
8. Did the waves wash Captain Carlsen overboard?
9. Was it January 8th now?
10. Was it now three weeks since the accident?

Exercise 50 — Put into the Past Tense (page 22)

1. It is now two weeks since the accident.
2. At the stern, the cable starts rubbing over sharp metal.
3. Every two hours, one of the men scrambles along to look at it.
4. Once, Captain Carlsen takes a pound of butter with him.
5. He smears the butter on the cable.

6. He feels a bit silly as he does so. *(Two verbs!)*
7. But he thinks it may help. *(Two verbs!)*
8. He doesn't want the cable to break.

Exercise 51 – Either/Or (pages 22–24)

1. Did Captain Carlsen put the butter on his bread or on the cable?
2. Did he feel very clever, or a bit silly?
3. Did the men get wet on the deck or in the cabin?
4. Did they try to dry their clothes on the deck or in the cabin?
5. Did the King of Denmark want to give a medal to Captain Carlsen or to Mr Dancy?
6. Did the Danish government order a helicopter or a plane?
7. Did the plane fly to England or to the *Flying Enterprise?*
8. Is Falmouth in England or in Denmark?
9. Was the *Flying Enterprise* in front of the *Turmoil* or behind her?
10. Did the weather get better, or did it get worse?

Exercise 52 – Vocabulary (pages 21–24)

1. What is a word for *to go on foot, but not run*?
2. What is the opposite of *after*?
3. What is the opposite of *in front*?
4. What is another word for *to go on*?
5. What is the opposite of *always*?
6. What is one word for *next to*?
7. What do we call a *machine that can carry people through the air*?
8. What is the name for a *flying-machine with a rotor on top*?
9. What is another word for *journalists*?
10. What do we call a *picture taken with a camera*?
11. What is the name for a *special box which shows moving pictures*?
12. What is another word for *to talk about* a question?
13. What is the opposite of *better*?
14. What is the name for *the day before Wednesday*?
15. What is the word for *seven days*?
16. What do we call *something bad that happens by chance*?
17. What is another word for *foolish* or *stupid*?
18. What is the opposite of *dry*?
19. What is a word meaning *to pull (a ship, a car) behind you*?
20. What do we call *water falling from the sky*?

Exercise 53 – Describing a Picture (page 23)

1. What can you see in the picture on page 23?
   Write at least five longer sentences, as in Exercises 29 and 39.

Exercise 54 — Did You Understand Chapter 10? (pages 21–24)

1. How fast did the two ships sail?
2. Why didn't they sail faster?
3. What would happen if they sailed too slowly?
4. What was the weather like, in the next few days?
5. Why did the destroyer shoot a rope over to the ship?
6. Why did the helicopter circle over the ships?
7. Why did reporters come from Denmark?
8. What did the newspapers and radio do?
9. What did people think of Captain Carlsen?
10. What was the weather like now, out in the Atlantic?
11. What was the problem with the cable?
12. Why did Captain Carlsen smear butter on the cable?
13. Why couldn't the men dry their clothes?
14. Why did the Danish government order a special plane?
15. What happened in the middle of the night?

Exercise 55 — Short Answers (pages 24–25) **CHAPTER 11**

1. Was it half past one in the afternoon?
2. Was the ship fifty-three miles from Falmouth?
3. Was everything dark?
4. Were the waves big?
5. Did the tug send a message?
6. Will they have to wait till daylight?
7. Was the *Flying Enterprise* drifting towards England?
8. Could the *Turmoil* stop her?
9. Was the funnel under the water now?
10. Could the two men catch the rope from the tug?

Exercise 56 — Put into the Present Tense (page 25)

1. The *Flying Enterprise* was helpless.
2. The *Turmoil* couldn't stop her drifting.
3. Soon morning came, and it got light. *(Two verbs!)*
4. Mr Dancy looked at the funnel.
5. Now it was only just above the waves.
6. The tug came nearer to the *Flying Enterprise.*
7. The crew shot a rope across to the ship.
8. But waves were breaking all across the ship's decks.
9. The two men couldn't reach the rope.
10. It seemed impossible.
11. The weather was now too bad.

Exercise 57 — Either/Or (page 25)

1. Was the *Flying Enterprise* drifting towards England or away from England?
2. Did Mr Dancy look at the funnel or at the ship's tail?
3. Did reaching the rope seem easy or impossible?
4. Did the gale grow stronger or weaker during the night?
5. Did the men stay in their cabin, or did they move to another cabin?
6. Did Mr Dancy walk out of the cabin on January 10th, or did he climb out?

Exercise 58 — Put into the Past Tense (page 25)

1. The door of the new cabin is above the men's heads.
2. They hang up their hammocks and climb in. *(Two verbs!)*
3. All the time, the wind goes on blowing.
4. More and more water is washing into the ship.
5. The next morning, Mr Dancy goes out of the cabin.
6. He has to climb up a rope to get out.
7. He sees the funnel down on the water.
8. He tells Captain Carlsen that the ship is sinking. *(Two verbs!)*

Exercise 59 — Mixed Questions (pages 24–25)

1. How far was the *Flying Enterprise* from England?
2. What message did the tug send?
3. When did the tug come nearer and shoot a rope across?
4. Who had to move to a new cabin?
5. Where was this new cabin?
6. Where was the door of the new cabin?
6. How did Mr Dancy get out of the cabin?
7. What was breaking into the funnel?

Exercise 60 — Vocabulary (pages 24–25)

1. What is the opposite of *nothing*?
2. What is the word for *information that you send to someone*?
3. What do we call the *first part of the day, up to 12 o'clock*?
4. What is the word for the *chimney of a ship*?
5. What is the opposite of *floor*?
6. What is the opposite of *last*?

Exercise 61 — Put into the Past Tense (pages 25–27) **CHAPTER 12**

1. The funnel is dipping in the water now.
2. The two men have to climb up higher and higher.
3. They climb along the funnel.

4. The ship has turned right over onto her side.
5. So Mr Dancy jumps into the water first.
6. One minute later, Captain Carlsen follows him.

Exercise 62 — Short Answers (pages 25–27)

1. Are the two men abandoning ship?
2. Did the ship sink lower in the water?
3. Was the gale terribly strong?
4. Did the men have to climb higher up the ship?
5. Was water rushing into the *Willard Keith*?
6. Did both men jump into the water?
7. Was Mr Dancy the last to leave the ship?

Exercise 63 — Either/Or (page 27)

1. Did the men climb along the funnel or into a cabin?
2. Was water coming into the funnel fast or slowly?
3. Did the men jump from the funnel or from the deck?
4. Did they jump together or one after the other?
5. Were the men taken on board the tug or the destroyer?

Exercise 64 — Mixed Questions (pages 25–27)

1. Who did the men send a message to?
2. What did the men have to get away from?
3. Who was the first to jump?
4. When did Captain Carlsen jump?
5. How long had Captain Carlsen fought for his ship?
6. Where were the men when the *Turmoil* sailed into Falmouth?

Exercise 65 — Describing a Picture (page 26)

1. What can you see in the picture on page 26?
   Write at least five longer sentences, as in Exercises 29, 39 and 53.

Exercise 66 — Did You Understand Chapters 11 & 12? (pages 24–27)

1. Where was the *Flying Enterprise* at the beginning of Chapter 11?
2. Why did they have to wait for daylight?
3. Why couldn't the two men reach the rope from the tug?
4. Why couldn't the men stay in their cabin?
5. How did they get in and out of their new cabin?
6. What made Captain Carlsen say, "It's almost time for us to go"?
7. What message did they send to the other ships?
8. What part of the ship did they jump from?
9. Why did they jump from there?
10. Why did Mr Dancy jump first?

Asking Questions

These exercises are intended for classes with little practice in formulating questions of their own. They offer a progression of gradually increasing difficulty, moving to a mixture of auxiliary-inversions and use of periphrastic 'did', both with and without question words, by the end of Chapter 12. Questions using 'do' and 'does' are not covered in this material.

Such structured progression may offer important support for weaker pupils; as always, the material can be altered or augmented according to the needs of the class. The introductory phrase "Ask your teacher ..." can, of course, refer just as well to a guest, a classmate or anyone else considered suitable for the role!

Chapter 1

Ask your teacher ...

1. ... if it *was* Christmas Eve.
2. ... if the weather *was* icy-cold.
3. ... if a strong wind *was* blowing.
4. ... if a ship *was* sailing from Hamburg to America.
5. ... if she *was* carrying a lot of cargo.
6. ... if there *were* eleven passengers.
7. ... if the passengers *were* travelling to America.
8. ... if there *were* two children among them.

Chapter 2

Ask your teacher ...

1. ... if the sailors *can* mend the crack.
2. ... if they *can* stop the water coming in.
3. ... if the ship *will* get to America safely.
4. ... if the storm *will* soon be over.
5. ... if the ship *is* going to sink.
6. ... if the passengers *will* all be drowned.
7. ... if this *is* a terrible storm.
8. ... if the people on the ship *must* keep calm.
9. ... if the sailors *are* working hard.
10. ... if they *are* doing their best.

Chapter 3

Ask your teacher ...

1. ... if the deck *is* flat now.
2. ... if the ship *will* turn right over.
3. ... if the crew *can* steer the ship.
4. ... if water *is* coming into the hold.
5. ... if they *are* sinking.

6. ... if there *were* three other ships nearby.
7. ... if everyone *must* leave the ship now.
8. ... if they *can* use the lifeboats.
9. ... if they *will* have to jump into the sea.
10. ... if the water *was* like ice.

Chapter 4

Ask your teacher ...

1. ... if another ship *arrived* now.
2. ... if the American captain *called* to Captain Carlsen.
3. ... if the helpless ship *drifted* northwards.
4. ... if her steering no longer *worked*.
5. ... if the news *surprised* the sailors.
6. ... if Captain Carlsen *ordered* a tug to salvage his ship.
7. ... if the tug *waited* only twenty minutes at Falmouth.
8. ... if the tug *sailed* at once for the North Atlantic.
9. ... if the American sailors *looked* at Captain Carlsen's ship.
10. ... if Captain Carlsen *waved* to the American destroyer.

Chapter 5

Ask your teacher ...

1. ... if Captain Carlsen *stood* on the wall of his cabin.
2. ... if he *sent* a message to the destroyer.
3. ... if he *told* his wife not to worry.
4. ... if an answer *came* from the destroyer.
5. ... if night *fell*.
6. ... if huge waves *began* to batter the ship.
7. ... if the captain *found* a candle.
8. ... if the captain *slept* much.
9. ... if he *had* to do without tea.
10. ... if he *drank* some lemonade.

Chapter 6

Ask your teacher ...

1. ... if the hours *went* by.
2. ... if Captain Carlsen *had* nothing hot to eat.
3. ... if the sailors *fired* the gun.
4. ... if the rope *flew* across the waves.
5. ... if Captain Carlsen *tried* to catch it.
6. ... if the ship's decks *sloped* very steeply.
7. ... if Captain Carlsen *missed* the rope.
8. ... if the rope *fell* into the water.

9. ... if Captain Carlsen *tied* the fourth rope to a rail.
10. ... if he *caught* the box at last.

Chapter 7

Ask your teacher ...

1. ... if the tug *began* work immediately.
2. ... if the tug *had* big, strong lights.
3. ... if the crew *had* a special rope-gun.
4. ... if the ship *was* listing badly.
5. ... if the crew *could* see the ship's broken rudder.
6. ... if Captain Carlsen *needed* help.
7. ... if the tug *sailed* nearer to the ship.
8. ... if Captain Carlsen *was* holding onto the rails.
9. ... if the ship *was* nearly on her side.
10. ... if the tug *could* get the ship to England.

Chapter 8

Ask your teacher ...

1. ... if something *happened* that seemed impossible.
2. ... if the tug *bumped* against Captain Carlsen's ship.
3. ... if Mr Dancy *saw* his chance.
4. ... if he *grabbed* the rail with both hands.
5. ... if he *hung* from the ship's stern.
6. ... if the waves *broke* over him.
7. ... if Mr Dancy *landed* on board the ship.
8. ... if he *scrambled* up the deck.
9. ... if Captain Carlsen *smiled* at him.
10. ... if the two men *shook* hands.

Chapter 9

Ask your teacher ...

1. ... if the waves *were* enormous.
2. ... if waves *came* crashing onto the ship.
3. ... if water *washed* around the two men.
4. ... if it *grew* dark.
5. ... if the men *climbed* through the door of the cabin.
6. ... if Mr Dancy *saw* the captain's hammock.
7. ... if there *was* some cake in the hammock.
8. ... if Mr Dancy *liked* cake.
9. ... if the men *can* hang up a hammock for Mr Dancy.
10. ... if Mr Dancy *must* wear a lifejacket.

Chapter 10

Ask your teacher ...

1. ... where the American destroyer *sailed* now.
2. ... what it *shot* over to Captain Carlsen.
3. ... what the sailors *could* send to the two men.
4. ... where the helicopter *flew* out from.
5. ... who the helicopter *was* carrying.
6. ... where the helicopter *circled.*
7. ... what the reporters *took.*
8. ... what the plane *did.*
9. ... what the newspapers *were* full of.
10. ... what millions of people *listened* to.

Chapter 11

Ask your teacher ...

1. ... what time it *was.*
2. ... what the tug *sent.*
3. ... what they *will* have to wait for.
4. ... what Mr Dancy *looked* at, when morning came.
5. ... where the tug *shot* a rope.
6. ... why the men *couldn't* reach the rope.
7. ... how they *tried* to catch the rope.
8. ... why the two men *couldn't* stay in their cabin.
9. ... where they *moved* to.
10. ... what Mr Dancy *saw* on Thursday morning.

Chapter 12

Ask your teacher ...

1. ... if the men *sent* a message to the other ships.
2. ... what the funnel *was* doing now.
3. ... why the men *had* to climb up higher.
4. ... if they *climbed* along the funnel.
5. ... where the water *was* rushing in fast.
6. ... where the men *stood* before they jumped.
7. ... if the captain *wanted* to jump first.
8. ... when Mr Dancy *jumped* into the sea.
9. ... if the waves *are* breaking over the sinking ship.
10. ... when the tug *sailed* into the port of Falmouth.

Retelling the Story

When you have worked on a chapter, you can try retelling parts of the story orally in class. Sometimes you may need only three or four sentences, but some of the suggested topics will be a little longer. One thing is important, though: you mustn't read what you say to the class, and you mustn't have any book or paper in front of you when you speak. If you feel really nervous and think that you must have a paper, give it to the teacher, who can help if necessary.

The line references show you where to start and stop: "3,1" means "page 3, line 1".

Chapter 1:	1.	Christmas Eve, 1951 – How the story began (3,1–3,15)
	2.	The night and the next morning (3,16–4,3)
Chapter 2:	1.	Trying to mend the crack (4,4–4,19)
	2.	How the ship rolled over (4,24–6,12)
Chapter 3:	1.	How the other ships arrived (6,17–7,2)
	2.	Leaving the ship (7,2–7,15)
Chapter 4:	1.	The *Turmoil* (9,22–9,32)
	2.	How the American sailors watched the ship (10,6–10,18)
Chapter 5:	1.	Captain Carlsen's radio (10,23–12,4)
	2.	Cold and thirsty (12,14–12,23)
Chapter 6:	1.	Shooting the rope (14,8–14,21)
	2.	A box for Captain Carlsen(14,22–16,4)
Chapter 7:	1.	The *Turmoil* (16,21–16,27)
	2.	Ropes and cables (16,27–17,13)
Chapter 8:	1.	Trying to fix the rope (17,23–18,16)
	2.	Something impossible (18,17–18,31)
Chapter 9:	1.	In the cabin (20,11–20,27)
	2.	How they fixed the cable (20,28–21,12)
Chapter 10:	1.	How the ship became famous (22,1–22,18)
	2.	Problems with the cable, Part I (22,25–22,32)
	3.	Problems with the cable, Part II (24,14–24,24)
Chapter 11:	1.	Trying to fix the cable again (24,25–25,11)
	2.	The last night and the last morning (25,12–25,24)
Chapter 12:	1.	Abandoning ship (25,25–27,11)
	2.	The rescue and the return to England (27,11–27,23)

List of English Irregular Verbs

Introduction

Here is a list of the most important irregular verbs in English. They are arranged, not alphabetically, but in 'sound families', as experience has shown this to facilitate learning. Most classes will aim to have achieved an excellent knowledge, both oral and written, of the whole list by the end of Class 8; at earlier stages, selection of what is to be learned is a matter for the individual teacher.

Offering the complete list here, then, enables the teacher to select according to the specific needs of the class, while at the same time giving each pupil an overview of the material to be covered in the course of the Middle School.

The 51 irregular verbs occurring in the main text of this reader are marked with an asterisk before the verb number.

GROUP 1 – BEGIN					
*	1.	to begin	began	begun	anfangen
	2.	to spring	sprang	sprung	(plötzlich) springen
*	3.	to sing	sang	sung	singen
	4.	to ring	rang	rung	läuten, anrufen
	5.	to swim	swam	swum	schwimmen
*	6.	to drink	drank	drunk	trinken
*	7.	to sink	sank	sunk	sinken, versenken
	8.	to stink	stank	stunk	stinken
GROUP 2 – CLING					
	9.	to cling	clung	clung	s. klammern, festhalten
	10.	to sting	stung	stung	stechen
	11.	to fling	flung	flung	schleudern
*	12.	to swing	swung	swung	schwingen, schwenken; baumeln
	13.	to wring	wrung	wrung	(aus)wringen
*	14.	to hang	hung	hung	(auf)hängen
			(hanged = henkte, erhängt!)		
	15.	to spin	spun	spun	s. drehen; *(Garn)* spinnen
	16.	to dig	dug	dug	graben
	17.	to stick	stuck	stuck	(an)stecken, ankleben
	18.	to strike	struck	struck	schlagen, treffen
	19.	to win	won	won	gewinnen
GROUP 3 – SLEEP					
*	20.	to sleep	slept	slept	schlafen
	21.	to creep	crept	crept	kriechen
	22.	to sweep	swept	swept	fegen, kehren
*	23.	to keep	kept	kept	behalten

	24. to weep	wept	wept	weinen
	25. to meet	met	met	treffen, begegnen
*	26. to feel	felt	felt	(s.) fühlen
	27. to kneel	knelt	knelt	knien
	28. to bleed	bled	bled	bluten
	29. to feed	fed	fed	füttern
	30. to flee	fled	fled	fliehen
	31. to lead	led	led	führen
*	32. to leave	left	left	weggehen, verlassen
*	33. to hold	held	held	halten
	34. to deal	dealt	dealt	handeln, s. befassen mit
	35. to mean	meant	meant	bedeuten
	36. to lean	leant	leant	(s.) lehnen
	37. to dream	dreamt	dreamt	träumen
	38. to read	read	read	lesen

GROUP 4 – LEARN (ALLE VERBEN DIESER GRUPPE GEHEN AUCH MIT -ED STATT MIT -T!)

*	39. to burn	burnt (burned)	burnt (burned)	(ver)brennen
	40. to learn	learnt (learned)	learnt (learned)	lernen
	41. to smell	smelt (smelled)	smelt (smelled)	riechen
	42. to spell	spelt (spelled)	spelt (spelled)	buchstabieren
	43. to spoil	spoilt (spoiled)	spoilt (spoiled)	verderben
	44. to spill	spilt (spilled)	spilt (spilled)	verschütten

GROUP 5 – SEND

	45. to bend	bent	bent	biegen, beugen
	46. to lend	lent	lent	(ver)leihen
*	47. to send	sent	sent	schicken, senden
	48. to spend	spent	spent	*(Geld)* ausgeben; *(Zeit)* verbringen
*	49. to build	built	built	bauen

GROUP 6 – FIND

*	50. to find	found	found	finden
	51. to bind	bound	bound	binden
	52. to grind	ground	ground	mahlen; schleifen
	53. to wind	wound	wound	winden

GROUP 7 – THINK

	54. to buy	bought	bought	kaufen
	55. to bring	brought	brought	bringen
*	56. to think	thought	thought	denken
*	57. to fight	fought	fought	kämpfen
*	58. to catch	c*au*ght	c*au*ght	fangen
	59. to teach	t*au*ght	t*au*ght	lehren, unterrichten

GROUP 8 – WRITE

	60. to drive	drove	driven	fahren
*	61. to rise	rose	risen	aufgehen *(Sonne);* s. erheben
	62. to write	wrote	written	schreiben
	63. to ride	rode	ridden	reiten

GROUP 9 – SHOOT

*	64. to get	got	got	bekommen; werden
	65. to forget	forgot	forgotten	vergessen
*	66. to shoot	shot	shot	schießen
	67. to shine	shone	shone	scheinen, glänzen
	68. to lose	lost	lost	verlieren

GROUP 10 – SPEAK

*	69. to speak	spoke	spoken	sprechen
	70. to steal	stole	stolen	stehlen
*	71. to break	broke	broken	(zer)brechen
	72. to freeze	froze	frozen	frieren, gefrieren
	73. to wake up	woke up	woken up	aufwachen; -wecken
*	74. to tell	told	told	erzählen, sagen
	75. to sell	sold	sold	verkaufen
	76. to choose	chose	chosen	(aus)wählen

GROUP 11 – WEAR

	77. to wear	wore	worn	*(Kleider)* tragen
	78. to tear	tore	torn	zerreißen
	79. to swear	swore	sworn	schwören, fluchen
	80. to bear	bore	borne (born = geboren!)	ertragen

GROUP 12 – HIDE

	81. to hide	hid	hidden	(s.) verstecken
	82. to bite	bit	bitten	beißen
*	83. to light	lit (lighted)	lit (lighted)	anzünden
	84. to slide	slid	slid	gleiten, rutschen

GROUP 13 – 'W' VERBS

	85. to know	knew	known	kennen, wissen
*	86. to blow	blew	blown	wehen, blasen
*	87. to grow	grew	grown	wachsen; werden
	88. to throw	threw	thrown	werfen
*	89. to fly	flew	flown	fliegen
	90. to draw	drew	drawn	zeichnen; ziehen
	91. to show	showed	shown	zeigen
	92. to sow	sowed	sown	säen
	93. to sew	sewed	sewn	nähen
	94. to saw	sawed	sawn	sägen

GROUP 14 – CUT

95.	to bet	bet	bet	wetten
96.	to broadcast	broadcast	broadcast	senden, ausstrahlen *(Radio/TV)*
97.	to burst	burst	burst	bersten, platzen
98.	to cost	cost	cost	kosten
99.	to cut	cut	cut	schneiden
*100.	to hit	hit	hit	treffen, schlagen
101.	to hurt	hurt	hurt	weh tun; verletzen
*102.	to let	let	let	(zu)lassen
*103.	to put	put	put	stellen, setzen, legen
104.	to set	set	set	setzen; untergehen *(Sonne)*
105.	to shut	shut	shut	schließen
106.	to spread	spread	spread	ausbreiten, ausdehnen; *(aufs Brot)* streichen
107.	to thrust	thrust	thrust	stoßen

GROUP 15 – AUXILIARY VERBS

*108.	to be	was / were	been	sein
*109.	to have	had	had	haben
*110.	to do	did	done	tun

GROUP 16 – REMAINING VERBS

*111.	to make	made	made	machen
*112.	to go	went	gone	gehen, fahren
*113.	to come	came	come	kommen
*114.	to become	became	become	werden
*115.	to run	ran	run	laufen, rennen
*116.	to see	saw	seen	sehen
*117.	to hear	heard	heard	hören
*118.	to give	gave	given	geben
119.	to forgive	forgave	forgiven	vergeben
120.	to forbid	forbade	forbidden	verbieten
*121.	to say	said	said	sagen
122.	to pay	paid	paid	bezahlen
123.	to lay	laid	laid	legen
*124.	to lie	lay	lain	liegen
*125.	to sit	sat	sat	sitzen
*126.	to stand	stood	stood	stehen
127.	to understand	understood	understood	verstehen
*128.	to beat	beat	beaten	schlagen
*129.	to take	took	taken	nehmen
*130.	to shake	shook	shaken	schütteln
*131.	to eat	ate	eaten	essen
*132.	to fall	fell	fallen	fallen